Cowboy Trout

Cowboy Trout

WESTERN FLY FISHING AS IF IT MATTERS

Paul Schullery

Montana Historical Society Press

Helena, Montana

Front cover art: *Mirage*, by Monte Dolack, © 1993
Frontispiece: Courtesy Mike Korn

Book design by Bob Smith, UpperWest Creative
Typeset in Sabon
Printed in Canada by Friesens

Distributed by the Globe Pequot Press, 246 Goose Lane, Guilford,
Connecticut 06437 (800) 243-0495

06 07 08 09 10 11 12 13 14 15   11 10 9 8 7 6 5 4 3 2 1

ISBN-13 978-0-9721522-7-3
ISBN-10 0-9721522-7-X

Library of Congress Cataloging-in-Publication Data

Schullery, Paul.
  Cowboy trout : western fly fishing as if it matters / Paul Schullery.
     p. cm.
  Includes bibliographical references and index.
  ISBN-13: 978-0-9721522-7-3 (pbk. : alk paper)
  ISBN-10: 0-9721522-7-X (pbk. : alk paper)
  1. Trout fishing—West (U.S.) 2. Fly fishing—West (U.S.) I. Title.
  SH 688.U6S38 2006
  799.12'4—dc22

                                                   2005035662

For Dale Greenley

This book was made possible in part
by funding from the Bair Trust.

Contents

Some sixteenth-century British anglers enjoyed tying a pike by its tail to the foot of a goose, happily regarding the ensuing struggle as good "sport." The values and definitions of sport have changed substantially since then, and continue to change today.

Fred Buller and Hugh Falkus, *Falkus and Buller's Freshwater Fishing* (1975; rev. ed., London: Stanley Paul, 1988), p. 124

Can Fly Fishing Make You a Westerner?

More fundamentally, the West plays West, and acts out a kind of Easterner's view of the West based more on the testimony of television than of history, because the West has become Eastern; the Westerner has become an Easterner, and not merely host to Easterners.

—Earl Pomeroy, *In Search of the Golden West* (1957)

In the 1659 edition of *The Art of Angling*, Thomas Barker (who described himself as "an antient practitioner in the said Art") explained the "principall sport" of fishing for pike. It was a method startling in its originality—Barker said that it was "the greatest pleasure that a noble Gentleman in Shropshire giveth his friends for entertainment." The goal was to snag a pike with a very large bare hook, and the "sport" arose from tying the other end of the line to a goose. The two animals would then tear up the pond—towing each other around in a blind panic—apparently to the vast entertainment of the noble gentlemen. At least Barker assured his readers that "there is no doubt of pleasure betwixt the Goose and the Pike."[1]

2 ~ Cowboy Trout

Well maybe, but not for the goose or the pike. It must have been terrifying for them. And yet, I suspect that even today, when most of us would agree that such awful treatment of animals is nothing short of immoral, and when *almost* all of us would be unwilling to snag the pike in the first place, there are some among us who wouldn't mind seeing such a contest—maybe, just once. As terrible a thing as it was, perhaps, late at night when our resistance is down, it still has a certain barbaric appeal—like professional wrestling, or Jerry Springer—even though we know better.

Sport changes that way, with rarely a perfect break from the past. Sport's evolution is as sloppy and troubled as any other social process. We don't all get together one day and abruptly agree that we need to do things differently. Some of us grow uneasy about something, and gradually we give it up. Eventually, if many people get to feeling strongly about it, a new code of behavior emerges. If the code has sufficient emotional urgency and political momentum, it becomes law. Sometimes these changes start slowly, or languish for a long time, or even die out. Other times, there's a sudden sense of urgency, things reach a flash point, and we look around and realize we're not who we used to be.[2]

One fall day about thirty years ago, I was driving along the North Umpqua River in Oregon when I saw a fly fisherman on the opposite shore playing a steelhead (a sea-going form of rainbow trout that returns to fresh water to spawn). I pulled over and got out to watch. Just as the fish was tiring, another car pulled up and four men got out and joined me.

The fisherman worked the steelhead into the shallows

and gently gripped it underneath. It looked to be a ten-pound fish, sleek and bright. The fisherman quickly worked the hook free and held the fish in the shallow water for a moment, admiring it.

But when he aimed the fish back toward the deep water and eased it to freedom, a chorus of gasps rose from the men near me. They walked back to their car shaking their heads. As the last one turned to go, he snorted and said, "He must be one of them *sportsmen*."

What engages my interest here is not if the fisherman should have let the fish go or if the men were wrong in disapproving of him. What is more interesting is what the situation reveals about angling society and its internal complications. The fisherman returned a fish to the river, a big strong fish that any one of these men might very well catch the next day. It would seem he did them a favor. But the continued availability of that fish was less important to them than the statement that the fisherman was silently making about his definition of sport—and, by implication, about theirs.

The man who made the sarcastic remark about "them sportsmen" was speaking against a movement more than against an individual. It was a telling moment for me because up until then I didn't fully realize that such hostilities existed within the so-called "fraternity" of anglers. Those hostilities were part of a very important change in trout fishing that was just then gaining new national momentum—a movement away from the gratuitous harvest of every good fish you caught. The fisherman and the watchers were all a part of that change, he as a convert, they as the resistance.

What also appeals to me about stories like this one, and the previous one about the pike and the goose, is the extent to which this whole messy business of angling society—its debates, its value systems, and its unceasing change—is ripe for our consideration, our introspection, and our enrichment. For a variety of reasons, I think that ripeness is especially attractive and promising here in the West.

In 1977, I left my occasional job as a Yellowstone National Park ranger-naturalist to move to Vermont and work for the American Museum of Fly Fishing. In my naive way, I had an ambition for this splendid little institution. My years in the West convinced me that this profoundly eastern museum needed to pay more attention to western fishing traditions. I worried that the easterners would resist that, but it turned out that the problem wasn't the easterners. The problem was that most western anglers were happily oblivious of their own history, traditions, and folklore. More than once back then I heard western fly fishers say, "We don't have any history in the West; we're just making it now."

This was an interesting perspective, in part because it suggested that the western angler saw himself (they were almost all male) as a kind of pioneer, boldly starting something new on a real frontier. In a hundred ways, the popular image of the West as a place of great newness and opportunity and freedom supported that thinking.

At the same time, it was disappointing, even amazing, that these people really did believe that they had somehow just recently materialized in an utterly ahistorical context—that there was no yesterday in western fly fishing. The

West's remarkable fishing history was virtually unknown and was apparently in danger of being lost.

The first eastern American book devoted entirely to fly fishing was written by a New York newspaper columnist named George Dawson. It was called *Pleasures of Angling*, and it was published in 1876. The first *western* American book devoted solely to fly fishing was written by a Denver attorney named Lewis B. France. It was called *With Rod and Line in Colorado Waters*, and it was published in 1884, only eight years after its eastern counterpart. The first book on fly fishing Yellowstone Park was published in 1910. Western fishing doesn't lack a history. It just lacks historians.

Among the fishermen, it is difficult to get anyone to pay attention to the sport's obscure or unknown past when so much is happening in the surprising present—especially the spectacular emergence of fly fishing as a fashionable thing to do.

I've expressed bewilderment over this startling development before—how it could happen that "this intensely personal and oddly tradition-oriented sport, so long the province of obsessive loners and snooty grouches, should become fashionable. Who could have predicted that?"[3] But we ratchet up the improbability meter another notch or two as we watch fly fishing become not only stylish in the West, but a shiny badge of regional authenticity—of a person's *westernness*. Where did *that* come from?

Of course it came from lots of places and had lots of causes. I intend to mention quite a few of them in this book. But I doubt that I'll settle much. If I thought there were sim-

*Kim Allen Scott, Special Collections librarian, left,
and Bruce Morton, dean of Libraries, examine a volume
in Montana State University's extensive and rapidly
growing trout and salmonid collection.*

Bärbel Morton, photographer, Special Collections,
Montana State University Libraries, Bozeman

ple answers to questions like these, I probably wouldn't bother to ask them. The historian's enterprise, like the fly fisher's, never has been especially conclusive.

And I'm pleased to see that the two enterprises are finally connecting in the West. Just take my neighborhood as an example.

In 1999, Montana State University, already known as "Trout U" both for the surrounding trout streams and for its involvement in fisheries research, launched an ambitious project to develop a world-class trout and salmonid library. In less than six years, the collection has exceeded 5,000 items and is approaching world class, if it has not already arrived.

In June 2000, the Museum of the Rockies in Bozeman hosted *Anglers All: Humanity at Midstream*, the traveling exhibit of the American Museum of Fly Fishing. Museum staff greatly broadened the exhibit by developing a colorful and thoughtful regional exhibit to accompany it, *The Lure and Lore of Western Waters*.[4] It was extraordinarily popular.

In May 2001, Montana State University presented Bud Lilly, native Montanan fly-fishing outfitter and conservationist, with an honorary doctorate, demonstrating, among other good things, that fly fishing has a great deal to do with good citizenship.

Parallel developments have been equally encouraging in the other state that I have considered home the past fifteen years, Wyoming. Adrian Bantjes, in the History Department at the University of Wyoming, recently taught what I assume is the first seminar on the history of fly fishing offered at any western university, perhaps at any American university,

Few events more clearly signaled the arrival of fly fishing as a noteworthy element of the western American social scene than the 2000 exhibit The Lure and Lore of Western Waters *at the Museum of the Rockies, Bozeman, Montana.*

Beth Merrick, photographer, Museum of the Rockies, Bozeman, Montana

requiring his students to research and write on the rich and almost entirely unstudied history of Wyoming's long fly-fishing experience. His students made much use of the splendid collection of early and modern fly-fishing books in the university's Toppan and LaFontaine Collections, and have produced a number of important papers and publications about Wyoming's fisheries management and fishing history.

Both Wyoming and Montana have recently highlighted fly-fishing history in their official historical publications as well. In the summer of 2002, *Montana The Magazine of Western History,* the widely admired journal of the Montana Historical Society, devoted an entire issue to fly-fishing history. Clark Whitehorn, *Montana's* editor and a fisherman himself, was actually able to find four academically trained historians—John Byorth, Pat Munday, Ken Owens, and me—who had been studying western fishing history and had (or

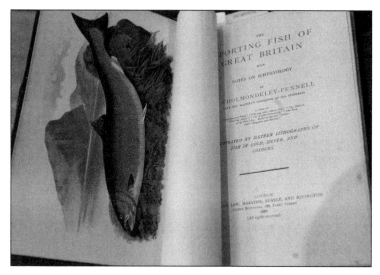

The Wyoming heritage of fly fishing, as venerable as that of any other western state, has inspired the development of the Toppan and LaFontaine Collections at the American Heritage Center, University of Wyoming, Laramie. Part of the Toppan Rare Books Library, these angling-related collections honor the memories of collectors Frederick and Clara Toppan and writer Gary LaFontaine, a long-time westerner and popular author of some of the most important modern fly-fishing texts.

Robert Hendricks, photographer, *Casper (Wyo.) Star-Tribune*

so we think) reasonably interesting things to say about it.[5]

In the winter of 2004, under the guest editorship of Adrian Bantjes, the fine magazine of the Wyoming State Historical Department, *Annals of Wyoming*, likewise produced a special issue related to the history of angling in that state.[6] The *Annals* special issue contained both conventionally researched essays (by Bantjes, Jeffrey Nichols, and me) and oral history (interviews of historically significant Wyoming angling figures by Adrian and Tucker Gallaway).

This is all very encouraging, even exhilarating, to the history-minded angler. Long the site of the extensive historical exhibits of the Fly Fishing Discovery Center (first in West Yellowstone, where it was known as the International Fly Fishing Center, and now in Livingston), as well as of tackle shops that are themselves both historic and objects of pilgrimage (Dan Bailey's, in Livingston, has for years devoted considerable floor space to a local history exhibit), Montana and its fly fishers display an interest in their history that is to one extent or another mirrored in other western states.

But, as long as I have hoped and worked for it, I don't view this elevating of fly fishing into the realm of Public Seriousness with unmixed feelings. For one thing, fly fishing's new status

The Federation of Fly Fishers, the sport's leading national organization, has long made the Yellowstone area its center of operations. Its Fly Fishing Discovery Center in Livingston, Montana, interprets ecology, angling, and conservation and is the Federation's foremost public presence.

Fly Fishing Discovery Center, Livingston, Montana

as an important thing is in good part the product of the fren-
zied promotion of western waters that has crowded me off
some of my favorite streams.

For another, I have some idea of what academic attention
means. It means good things, but such attention is never simple, and I doubt many of us are ready for what's coming.
Once we succeed in making fly fishing a legitimate subject
for broad intellectual inquiry, it's only a matter of time
before we're discovered by the shock troops of disciplines
who heretofore have been too busy frying other fish. Some
of this isn't going to be pleasant, much less exhilarating.

What, for example, will the environmental ethicists make
of our attitudes and our self-centered advocacies of preferred
fisheries management approaches? (I can tell you right now
that they're not going to be happy about the pike and goose.)

What will the ecofeminists—an entire productive school
of scholarship that most sportsmen have never heard of—
make of our comfortable worldview? (Let me go out on a
limb here and mention catch-and-release, just for a start.)

What will the ecological historians make of our brutally
successful overhauling of countless western aquatic ecosystems for the sake of better fishing?

In short, what will a whole hoard of very bright people,
concerned with a host of regional historical and social issues,
from race to gender to literature to industry to folklore to natural resource management, make of the tidy narratives we
have so lovingly constructed to explain ourselves to ourselves?

My greatest hope is that we get to find out. Because the
only thing worse than having all these people notice us and

The western fly fisher's self-perception as a pioneer on an
unfished frontier may never have been very accurate,
but it contributed to an enduring sense of regional identity
passed on from generation to generation. This young man
fished Montana's Big Hole River, circa 1958.

Bill Browning, photographer, Montana Historical Society
Photograph Archives, Helena

dissect us according to their very different lights would be to have them continue to ignore us.

Will they get us wrong sometimes? Sure thing; I know some of them well enough to predict just about where they'll go haring off on some agenda-fulfilling trail of their own that, in our view at least, misses the point, ignores or distorts the evidence, or is just stupid. But if we attract enough of their attention, it will reward us well for inviting them to notice us in the first place. There are many, many ways to perceive a trout—or a fly, for that matter. We fishermen are still a pretty complacent crowd at heart, and the twenty-first-century West is not an environment that nurtures complacency.[7]

The essays in this book represent the start I've tried to make at understanding the western fly fishers: where we came from, what we care about, and what our prospects are. I lean toward the northern Rockies and the Yellowstone region because that's what I've studied most. It's also where I've lived and fished most, hardly a coincidence.[8]

I likewise lean toward things I find especially appealing. Writers, amateur and professional, interest me, though I know their effect on the course of events is often negligible and usually overrated. On the other hand, there's nothing more important to the western angler than western water law, but the things I've written about it just haven't excited me as much as other subjects. Part of the book's open invitation into western fishing history is to be found in all the subjects it only brushes against, or leaves out entirely.

The hardest thing about writing these chapters was simultaneously sympathizing with the diverse audiences I most hope to reach. I'm a fisherman writing for fishermen, which means I want to tell fishing stories. Fishing writing, like any valuable writing, is really just one huge multi-generational conversation, all full of insights and foolishness and hero worship and complaints and wacky asides and ideas and adventures and hope; and in this book I take my turn in that conversation.

But I'm also a historian and naturalist, writing for other historians and naturalists. In my chosen stories, I'm trying to do what we do, too: advance a few theories, provide some examples of worthy study subjects, suggest some directions for further inquiry, and, again, tell a few stories. If I had to choose, I suppose I'd rather fail the fishermen than the academics, which probably means I won't satisfy either crowd.

Last, I wouldn't mind at all if this book also added a little to the fine tradition of angling books that celebrate fly fishing for the way it invites us into unfettered ecological settings and connects us to the wildness and wonder of rivers. Western fly fishing seems to me to raise to a new level of power the old saying that there is more to fishing than the catching of fish. The heightened sense of a wild place—not merely of the water, but of a whole landscape—has turned out to be fly fishing's greatest gift to me. For all the time I spend in libraries instead of on trout streams, I have never lost my certainty that being out there making new stories is always better than reading old ones.

Paul Schullery
on Matthew Bird Creek, spring 2006

In the summer of 1889, Rudyard Kipling encountered trout fishing of legenday proportions along the Yellowstone River south of Livingston. He said the river, "hidden by the water willows, lifted up its voice and sang a little song to the mountains."

From William Cullen Bryant, ed., *Picturesque America, or the Land We Live In*, 2 vols. (New York: D. Appleton, 1872), 1:292

CHAPTER ONE

"Ye Gods! That was fishing" An Old Sport Comes to the New West

There is, I think, not much point in being a fly-fisherman unless one is prepared to be generous and fairly relaxed about it.

—Roderick Haig-Brown, *A Primer of Fly Fishing* (1964)

On July 3, 1889, a young Rudyard Kipling, just then observing, writing, and fishing his way across the United States, stepped from the train in Livingston, Montana, which he quickly judged to be "a grubby little hamlet full of men without clean collars and perfectly unable to get through one sentence unadorned by three oaths."[1] But he loved the countryside, especially the Yellowstone River, which, "hidden by the water willows, lifted up its voice and sang a little song to the mountains." Later that day, as he was riding the park branch line south through Paradise Valley, a sympathetic stranger saw him eyeing the river and told him to "Lie off at Yankee Jim's if you want good fishing."[2] Kipling could not resist.

"Yankee Jim" George ran a toll road through the canyon now named for him, at the south end of Paradise Valley, and did a brisk business with tourists on their way to and from

Yellowstone National Park.[3] He also took in the occasional guest at his log hut overlooking the river. Kipling described him as "a picturesque old man with a talent for yarns that Ananias might have envied," but happily announced that he did not exaggerate the qualities of the river on those hot, sunny days:

> He said it was alive with trout. It was. I fished it from noon till twilight, and the fish bit at the brown hook as though never a fat trout-fly had fallen on the water. From pebbly reaches, quivering in the heat-haze where the foot caught on stumps cut four-square by the chisel-tooth of the beaver; past the fringe of water-willow crowded with the breeding trout-fly and alive with toads and watersnakes; over the drifted timber to the grateful shadow of the big trees that darkened the holes where the fattest fish lay, I worked for seven hours. The mountain flanks on either side of the valley gave back the heat as the desert gives it, and the dry sand by the railway track, where I found a rattlesnake, was hot-iron to the touch. But the trout did not care for the heat. They breasted the boiling river for my fly and they got it. I simply dare not give my bag. At the fortieth trout I gave up counting, and I had reached the fortieth in less than two hours. They were small fish,—not one over two pounds,—but they fought like small tigers, and I lost three flies before I could understand their methods of escape. Ye gods! That was fishing, though it peeled the skin from my nose in strips.[4]

Kipling and a generation of other anglers laid over at "Yankee Jim" George's cabin, pictured here in 1896, known for its rough accommodations and outstanding fishing in the canyon named for Yankee Jim, just a few miles north of Yellowstone National Park.

Montana Historical Society Photograph Archives, Helena

Rudyard Kipling was on his way from India to England and was soon to become one of the planet's most celebrated figures. He may seem anything but a typical man of his time, but in one way he was. Among serious fly fishers, he would have pretty much represented the average guy, and his tackle would have revealed just how cosmopolitan that average guy was.

His rod was probably made of "Calcutta" bamboo from India, split and glued into an excellent casting instrument by one of many British or American rod makers. His line was almost certainly silk from India or Persia, plaited to perfection in some European or American tackle factory. His leaders would have been silkworm gut from Italy, Sicily, Portugal, or (most likely) Spain. His flies could have contained feathers and furs from six continents, tied on Irish, English, or Norwegian hooks, in patterns representing several centuries of British fly-pattern theorizing.[5]

Kipling demonstrated that quite early in what we now might think of as the "frontier days," fly fishing in the "Wild West" was facilitated by a global trade, numerous multinational industries, and the efforts of individual laborers, craftsmen, and artisans in a dozen or more countries. Even in Kipling's time, when you fly fished the West, you brought the world with you.

When Kipling arrived in the West, most local anglers relied heavily on pre-existing techniques, equipment, and, especially, flies. But wherever they go, fly fishers soon begin to adapt.[6] Within decades, each western river would have its own local experts, its own favored local fly patterns, its own little set of sure-fire convictions—probably at least two or three competing schools of thought, in fact—about how best to catch its fish. As quickly, each river would generate its own heroes and its own stories, the essential trappings of culture.

This is what fishermen do. We bring our accumulated values, river savvy, hare-brained theories, technology, and improbable passions to new rivers and make the rivers our own. Within the limits set by our skills and tools, we exercise our sporting definitions and our aesthetic sensitivities to catch the new fish in the new place. Sometimes we further complicate the process by bringing old fish to the new place.

Yankee Jim's saloon provided modest indoor amenities in addition to scenery, fishing, and hunting in all directions.

Montana Historical Society Photograph Archives, Helena

The more generations that do these things, the more involved the tradition, and the more tangled the theoretical genealogy.

All these ideas and attitudes, more than our tackle or our cute little outfits, are what make each of us unique. To the average passer-by driving along some trout stream, we may all look to be stamped from the same cookie cutter, with our vests and rods and those leotard-style waders that are so fashionable now (I'm not quite that proud of my butt, thank you). But we each fish in our own little world of ideas, for our own private set of dreams.

I was reminded of our individuality one fall on the Madison River in Yellowstone Park, when I found myself fishing a rather too-famous stretch of the river with two other cookie cutters. We were all strangers to each other, but

*In his tackle, his methods, and his values, this modern fly fisher
on the Madison River still enjoys and displays the technical,
theoretical, and social baggage of several centuries of
European and American anglers.*

Courtesy the author

we were certainly alike in our determination. Though it was the brightest, most hopeless time of the day, and the word on the river was that there had been little action all week, we kept at it. Local etiquette dictated that each fisherman start at the head of the run and move downstream, wading along the shallow side and casting again and again across the river to the good water. I was first in line.

Perhaps because my family is of midwestern blue-collar bait-fishing stock, or maybe just because I lack a certain refinement in these matters, I often favor big flies—heavily weighted things that whistle threateningly past my ears when I cast. Most of the many hundreds of flies I carry in my vest are smaller and far trendier, but on the Madison, when legions of large brown trout are migrating past, I tend to move quickly from fashion to function. Big Woolly Buggers, Matukas, Montana Nymphs, and other disheveled, unruly things, each with a couple dozen turns of tin wire wrapped on the hook shank under the fly, sink fast into the deepest, most secure holds on the river. West Yellowstone guides and tackle dealers Craig Matthews and John Juracek say that the late Charlie Brooks, one of the early masters of this style of fishing, used to come in their shop, root through their selection of big flies, and announce that "These ain't ugly enough!"[7] Dredging such a fly through a promising run has for me a greater and edgier suspense than casting the prettiest, daintiest dry fly over the smoothest-rising trout in the river. The trout I can't see is always bigger than the one I can.

Just upstream from me was a traditionalist of the most quixotic sort. "I just don't enjoy casting all that weight," he told me, as he explained that he fished exclusively with soft-hackled wet flies. I recognized in him a type I especially admire, devoted to a gentle, unassuming purism expressed in elegant, simple little fly patterns, some hundreds of years old, fished across big water only a few inches beneath the surface. Constant mending of the line works these flies over the best spots at just the right pace. For me, a great part of the charm of his approach is that it requires you to fish so *persuasively* that the trout will be stirred to rise through several feet of fast water to take a morsel of food that, were it genuine, would barely fuel the effort. By comparison, in order for my crude, deeply fished flies to work, the trout has to do little more than open its mouth to get what it imagines to be a sizeable chunk of meat.

Upstream of the wet-fly man was our token hatch-matcher, studiously attentive to the prevailing insects on the water. There weren't many bugs in sight, but by studying the water for what might be going by, rolling river-bottom rocks to see which insects were most apparent, and experimenting with likely patterns, anglers of this type may have the highest odds of using a fly that imitates whatever the fish are actually looking for. This approach would seem intuitively superior to the others, and some hatch-matchers do imagine themselves to hold the intellectual (and even moral) high ground on many American and British trout streams these days. The fly-fishing magazines are full of their confident entomological treatises, far too many of which approach social bullying, implying that you can't be a *serious* fly fisher if you fish any other way. Still, I admire their approach, especially for its empirical commitment to understanding aquatic ecology rather than just mindlessly running some favorite but biologically bizarre fly through the water and asking the fish to forgive its shortcomings.

And yet each of us, in our own way, honored history and tradition. I could easily trace my big flies through at least two centuries of angling literature. Nineteenth-century British writers occasionally recommended flies (most intended for pike or saltwater fish, I admit) the size of a songbird. They sank them with lead, and made their eyes of beads, just as we do today. My streamers—imitating small fish that big fish like to eat—came to the Madison by way of early-twentieth-century landlocked-salmon waters in Maine, the bucktails swerving south through the heartland of the largemouth bass (or even farther, to the saltwater habitats of the Florida Keys), and the Matukas making an even longer detour through New Zealand. I was in good, if mixed, historical company.

My wet-fly companion just upstream had a much longer tradition to invoke. The soft-hackled fly he was casting, which owes much of its popularity in recent years to a series of helpful books by Montana writer Sylvester Nemes, is a product of the grand old "North Country tradition" of eighteenth- and nineteenth-century England.[8] They are also quite similar to fly patterns that appear continuously in the literature dating back to the thirteenth century, and by inference, almost two millennia. Medieval anglers, lacking our high-tech refinements and hip-hugging stylishness but urgently concerned with taking something home to eat, long ago recognized the effectiveness of a fly whose delicately barred feather barbules wave in the current as they drift past the trout.[9] These simple flies have always worked, and always will.

The hatch-matcher could likewise call upon a world of tradition to support his approach. The same two thousand years of angling wisdom has overwhelmingly endorsed using a fly that looks most like what the trout are eating. All three of us could claim to be doing that to some extent, of course, but the hatch-matcher was the only one whose imitative empiricism was front and center; an amazing number of modern fly fishers are proficient entomological taxonomists.

And this day on the Madison, their enthusiasms were vindicated, because the hatch-matcher was the only one among us to catch any fish. After a few fruitless rotations through the run, I took a seat up the slope a little ways, just to enjoy the sunshine and the comforting sight of well-cast fly lines gliding back and forth over the water. No sooner had I quit than the hatch-matcher's inquiries paid off, and he began to land fish. I was happy for him, but was also smugly relieved to see that they were smallish trout, not at all the ones that I was aiming for.

I could hear the hatch-matcher talking to the wet-fly man, who didn't seem to have anything to say in return, even when apparently offered a fly of the now-proven right pattern. He didn't especially want that fly, and I wasn't surprised. If the same offer had been made to me, I might at least have gone over to take a look at the fly, out of academic interest. I might even have made a few casts with it. But I'd soon have gone back to my own choices. The right fly must do more for me than catch fish, and this guy's right fly was pretty clearly not mine, whatever the fish thought. Angling history is largely a celebration of such idiosyncratic position-taking, just as it is a chronicle of the urge to feel superior about one's chosen idiosyncracies.

Alert fly fishers are not unaware of the peculiarity of their expertise. The loftiest literary celebrations of fly fishing tend to elevate this quirkiness—this profoundly personal passion we each develop about how we will fly fish—into a pseudo-Taoist catching/not-catching state of being in which the fish becomes less than the fishing, and the fisherman becomes one with some greater or finer something: the line, the fly rod manufacturer, the fly tier, the trout, the river, the watershed, the cosmos. The authors of these spiritual exclamations are in fact on to something important. I admit that there are parallels between a purely spiritual quest and the pursuit of unattainable perfection that fly fishing can become.

But beyond that, there are those of us who fear that the elevation of fly fishing into the realm of higher callings is a little too self-congratulatory, and at its worst gets kind of embarrassing. There may be a few among us who have indeed achieved some special state of being through fly fishing, but that doesn't justify the rest of us feeling so good about ourselves.

We fly fishers may have departed from our ancestors most significantly in the extent to which we feel compelled to treat our fly-fishing lives as redemption narratives, or coming-of-age tales, or just as straight-out substitutes for church attendance.

The river-as-church idea may be the most intriguing of these things. The association of the fishing life and the glory of God is nothing new in sport fishing, as even the casual reader of Izaak Walton knows, and as all readers of Norman Maclean's *A River Runs Through It* will also have noticed.[10] I'm not saying that fly fishers have gotten more religious, though for all I know they have. I am saying, instead, that maybe fly fishing has publicly taken on more of the trappings of a religion itself.

I could be wrong about this. It could be that all those generations of fly fishers before us, especially those who lived between, say, 100 A.D. and 1850 A.D., all had their share of souls looking for ever-higher jusifications for what they did with their fly rods. It could just be that it's only been lately that so many of us have been willing to admit this stuff, or have been able to write it down and get it published. After all, people who are passionate about nature-related pursuits of many kinds have long been suspected of turning those things into something like religion; we're not alone in attaching higher values to what we do out there.

Assigning the sport all these fancy metaphysical trimmings is mighty seductive, though, especially late at night when we get a little uneasy about having frittered away the best years of our lives on catching trout and are eager to give the whole business a little extra tone. My own hunch, based on thirty-some years with the trout and reading between the lines of several hundred fishing books, is that if you can't justify the fishing without invoking all these spiritual additives, you've probably missed the point. I still invoke them sometimes, but I try not to get too proud of it.

Fly fishing, in the West as everywhere else, is still pretty much just what Kipling showed us it was back when it was new here: an enchanting thing to do, enormously exciting while it happens, equally absorbing in the memories it leaves us, and—this may be the best thing about it—an inexhaustible source of dreams. Kipling must have found just such inspiration in the parting remark from his hosts in Yankee Jim Canyon: "An' you come back an' see us again," they said. "Come back an' we'll show you how to catch six-pound trout at the head of the cañon."[11]

In more than seventy years of fly fishing, fourth-generation Montanan Bud Lilly has seen fly fishing grow from "just something people did" to a badge of regional identity. His West Yellowstone Trout Shop, opened in 1950, has been a leading force in proving that fly fishing could also be big business in western recreation.

Mike Gurnett, photographer, Montana Fish, Wildlife and Parks, Helena

CHAPTER TWO

Fly Fishing in Western Culture

As laden with meaning as it is difficult to define, authenticity is, like the American West itself, a hotly contested and widely deployable concept in American culture.

—William R. Handley and Nathaniel Lewis, eds., *True West: Authenticity and the American West* (2003)

A few years ago, I spoke to a group at the University of Colorado. This was a pretty tweedy crowd, well informed on all the issues that confront the "New West." They were educated, thoughtful, and great fun. At the close of the evening's program, they were given time to ask me questions, and it was a remarkable process. One question would be about wolf recovery in the northern Rockies, and the next would be about why the Royal Coachman catches so many fish. When I got home, I couldn't wait to tell my friend Bud Lilly how thoroughly fly fishing seemed to be integrated into the intellectual fabric of my audience. When I did, Bud, who has been a leading figure in western angling for going on half a century now, said, "That's because fly fishing is part of our culture."

It wasn't like this was the first time I'd noticed that fly

fishing is pretty high profile out here in the West, but it did set me to wondering. Could something like fly fishing— which most people might regard as little more than a "leisure activity"—genuinely become a significant element of a region's culture? Or, to put the question another way, could fly fishing really be differently valued in the society of the West than in the society of the East, or the South, or any other region?

It is a charmingly, engagingly complex question, which in this essay I shall fail dismally to answer. But it is just the sort of question that a legitimate intellectual community should consider. We who fish in the West both need and deserve to build such a community. Fly fishing is great fun, and it is worth doing simply for that, but like any other significant human pursuit—music, art, cooking, gambling, literature, science, and religion all come to mind, and all, you might notice, are interwoven with fly fishing—it more or less demands our attention for other reasons, reasons that bring out the amateur anthropologist in all of us.

For the purposes of this discussion, let me set aside some very important questions. Most of all, let me set aside the controversial scholarly issue of just what culture is. Someone could fairly ask if fly fishing is culture at all, or if instead it is merely lifestyle. Someone *else* could then ask, "Well, if it's been a part of our regional lifestyle so long that it's become a tradition, and gathered about it all the trappings that go with sense of place, such as folklore, art, literature, and nat- ural-resource-based commerce, what is it if it isn't culture?" Fine. Those someones can ask those and many other ques- tions some other time. I dearly hope they will. But for the

Nationally known fishing writers, including Outdoor Life *writer Joe Brooks, shown here on Rock Creek near Missoula, Montana, brought western fly fishing to the attention of increasing numbers of traveling fishermen, especially in the 1960s and 1970s, when fly fishing experienced a regional and national boom in popularity.*

Bill Browning, photographer, Montana Historical Society
Photograph Archives, Helena

moment, I'm going to try to stick to other questions: Why is western fly fishing different, and why does it seem more important to its region?[1]

Many partial answers spring to mind. A terrific recreational

*Identification of the northern Rockies as a fly-fishing place
has been reinforced by countless commercial messages
in which fly fishing is used either as an enticement to visit
or just as an appropriate backdrop for advertising a wide
assortment of products and services.*

Travel Montana and photographer Tony Demin

industry must have something to do with it. The West has been a vacation destination for more than a century, and since the 1960s and the rise of the modern western ski industry, that sense of destination has increased. Fly fishing pretty clearly has ridden the coattails of a greater movement.[2]

But there are some disturbing implications in this line of thinking. People fly fish in great and excessive numbers in the East, but nobody back there thinks to use the sport in the East's defining iconography. For example, I don't know how a modern ad agency would choose to create a visual image of the typical easterner, but it's a cinch that the stereotype won't be holding a fly rod or wearing skis. Those things are done back there, but they don't define the region. Fly fishing has become, rather like forest fires and missile silos, one of the things that people in the East and other regions think of when they think of the West.

I don't know about you, but this looks to me like another example of that "colonial West" we used to hear so much about.[3] The question, I now realize, is who in fact has defined the West as a fly-fishing kind of place? And the answer is that, for the most part, it wasn't us. Many of the West's most ardent fly fishers, the ones who have talked and written the most about it, don't live here. Almost all of the leading local experts weren't born here.

This leads to even less savory thoughts about our regional sense of identity. Because it is probably true that many easterners don't see the West as having all that much meaningful culture anyway, we have to admit that they tend to think of the West as a place one goes to ski, or fly fish, or play cowboy, or watch wolves, or just be seen in the West. This raises another uneasy question: Is fly fishing so prominent in our regional culture just because we're so short on all the other things that New Yorkers regard as important? Is being thought of as a fly-fishing destination just a consolation prize for not measuring up in more important ways?

Or should we turn the eastern perspective back on itself and agree with *Fly Fisherman Magazine* editor John Randolph, who says that New York City is itself the most provincial place of all, and recognize the restorative sense of scale in a remark that fishing writer Charley Waterman once offered, that a two-foot-tall stained-glass window in New York would get more editorial comment than a year of South Dakota sunsets? Such thoughts may comfort us, but they will have no effect on the image-makers back east.

However we choose to go about it, and whatever we may think of the colonial implications, we are hard pressed *not* to define western fly-fishing culture by comparison with the East—just as the East, on those rare occasions when its fishermen might sense that they are not the point of the sport's origin either, must consider the Old World.

So, again, how is western fly fishing different?

Perhaps we could start with the fish. It has long been a matter of pride among western anglers that, though they suffered under what historian Patricia Limerick calls "the usual eastward tilt of historical significance," they at least still had the best fishing.[4] Eastern fly fishers, it was said, may have all that grand tradition of Thaddeus Norris, Theodore Gordon, Edward Hewitt, and all those other famous dead people in their historical pantheon, but here in the West, we still had streams worth fishing.

Of course that view is wrong twice. Not only do western anglers have an extraordinary history (of which they are sadly ignorant), but *eastern* anglers now have many streams managed well enough to rival the best wild trout fishing the West has to offer. So we have to look elsewhere than our lack of ancestor worship, or the superior numbers of our fish, to explain the rise of a distinct western fishing culture.

It's often helpful, and certainly entertaining, to hear from the cynics. The cynic might say that western fly fishing is so prominent for the very simple reason that white guys just got here later than they got to the East and haven't yet had time to ruin the fishing to the extent that they have in the East. After all, many hopeful voices to the contrary, western fly fishing is still primarily a pursuit of white male culture, that being only one of many "cultures" thriving in the West today. And prevailing environmentalist stereotypes have it that whatever is wrong with the health of the North American landscape is largely the fault of us white guys. Give us a little time, they would say, and we'll mess this up, too.

I agree that over the long haul, we white guys do have a dismal environmental record. Alfred Crosby, William Cronon, Patricia Limerick, and many other historians, including me, have provided the evidence to pretty well establish that. But considering how long the good fishing has endured and even been restored on many western waters, and considering that white guys are also restoring a lot of *eastern* waters, we have to admit, at least when it comes to fly fishing, that cynicism has lost some of its persuasiveness. Modern Americans, eastern and western, male or female, have shown a remarkable skill at preserving and restoring wild fisheries when they want to. They seem to want to more than ever before—not enough to suit me, but still quite a lot.

And for all the harm that has been done to western aquatic ecosystems with introduced fish species, diseases, overfishing, overcrowding, and industrial-scale degradation of many kinds, there is no denying that people from all over the world still want to come here to fish. We must be doing something right besides good marketing or that popularity wouldn't last. Western fly fishing is not a figment of the travel industry's imagination; it is still here, and it is still something special.

It is worth noting, however, that the cynics are already in full cry about the alleged quality of western fly fishing. My favorite of these skeptical souls is historian-novelist Ken Cameron, a longtime commentator on fly fishing's curious traditions. Ken wrote a stimulating attack on western fly fishing, published, ironically enough, in a stylish British fishing magazine, *Waterlog*. He based this attack on a trip he made to fish Montana's famous wild rivers.

Ken starts by describing Gallatin Field, near Bozeman, where his plane lands, as being overrun with annoying fly fishermen just like himself. He says it is "like a Masonic convention, with green cordura cases replacing red fezzes. I see one geezer (my age) showing another his rod. Many temptations to cheap Freudianism here."[5]

He continues, saying that the "airport is small but new,

This fly-fishing sculpture at Gallatin Field, the airport serving
the Bozeman, Montana, area, reflects the many fly fishers
en route to the region's famous waters.

Courtesy Ott Jones, sculptor

with a life-size statue of a fly-fisherman on the lawn outside, and inside a wall of ads for fishing outfitters and a scattering of what are called 'Western' bronzes—would-be Remingtons that cater to a supposedly Western taste for realism and kitsch. One is an Indian with a bow and arrow, who stares into the baggage area as if searching for something that hasn't arrived, or has already gone."[6]

After escaping the airport and various perceived inhospitalities in Livingston ("it might as well be Levittown for all the city planners care"), Ken takes a pack trip to the Absaroka backcountry, where he voices one of the most amazing and intellectually stimulating of complaints about wilderness fishing: that it is "unchallenging and somewhat stupid."[7] The native cut-throats are pretty, he admits, but small and too easy to catch.

Too easy to catch. This is the sort of phrase that in a properly tuned intellectual community should ignite all sorts of wonderful ruminations and dialogues. We could at least wonder at the egocentric aesthetic stance we human hunters and fishermen have developed, in which we have become the only predator species on earth that spends time worrying that our prey be worthy of our skills.

And then one wonders how many western chambers of commerce might actually feel the urge to apologize to Ken for the stupid fish, and promise him smarter ones if only he'll come back.[8]

Ken concludes with a description of Paradise Valley, south of Livingston: "It is depressing to find that the reality of a myth (true West, great trout) is one of inflated real estate, of luxury second houses pushing right up to the boundaries of the federal lands, of a self-conceived West that is being most insisted upon by people who have come here from other places."[9]

Then there's one last shot at Livingston, almost spookily echoing Kipling's comments about that town, quoted in the previous chapter:

> Our Livingston taxi driver is a woman who had begun life in Toldeo, Ohio. When I say that Montana is beautiful, she thanks me as if she is responsible for its creation. Yet the fact is that Livingston itself is a wretched little place with less real appeal than the Toledo she came from.[10]

Having lived for a few years in Livingston and knowing its history, I'd be inclined to say that Kipling was probably right, but that Ken should have looked around a little more. Although by this point in his trip, things had already progressed in a manner sufficiently unlike the advertisements that Ken apparently believed that nothing could look good to him except the plane home. So, as I imagine him in the rod-case parade filing onto an airplane at Gallatin Field, I wonder what catching a single twenty-two-inch brown trout might have done to his attitude about the West.

But Ken is making important points. We have all heard these complaints. We make them ourselves. They are in fact manifestations of changes now going on in western life generally, not just in fly fishing. They add to the welter of factors affecting the place of fly fishing in the regional society. And we still don't know why western fly fishing is different, even if there are now people, like Ken Cameron, who think that the only thing that matters about it is that it fails to honor its myth.

History can help us here. It can't calm down the cynics, but perhaps it can illuminate the source of the myth they find so elusive. The American West is well known to historians as a richly imagined region.[11] More than any other part of the country except perhaps Alaska (which many westerners now claim as part of their domain, presumably because it aggressively sustains its own set of myths about frontier life), the West is a national fantasy, a place where bigger, stranger, more heroic things are possible.[12]

But I'm not sure this western fishing myth is about imagination so much as it is about expectation. And when a new-comer arrives—inspired by a Roy Rogers–scale idea of some higher form of trout he is about to catch in a landscape that looks suspiciously like an old Marlboro billboard—we're no longer even dealing with expectations. We're dealing with demands. No wonder Ken required so much of the fishing and felt so strongly that he'd been sold a bill of goods.

History gives us other clues. While it might seem ironic that the West, the most arid portion of the nation, should be so disproportionately well known for its rivers, it is also true that a far higher portion of those rivers are in the public domain and therefore are, ideally at least, being managed for the use of everyone. Thanks to a raft of federal legislation, from the National Park Service Act and the Taylor Grazing Act to the Wilderness Act and the Endangered Species Act, there has long been some assurance of the survival of many reasonably robust and publicly accessible fisheries. Though many readers of Norman Maclean seem to admire him for celebrating some imagined social independence of the west-ern angler, we dare not forget that the public domain is the "It" that the river runs through. Eastern anglers are as much the legal proprietors of this landscape as are westerners. This inquiry gets messier all the time.

It is probably true that, for easterners and other outsiders at least, what makes western fly fishing special is found in a notion popular among scholars of tourism: it is prized for its "otherness." Generations of easterners, who for the first couple centuries of American fishing society and literature totally dominated the written record of the sport, did all this for us—or *to* us. They came out here, rode through the magnificent scenery of these high mountain drainages, breathed the cold wind slipping off snowfields, caught naive native trout by the ton, played cowboy a little bit, and then went home and firmed up the fantasy image of western fishing for all time to come.

It is tempting to describe western fly-fishing culture as a rare case of bioregionalism that was created not from within, but from without, sort of the way Jackson Hole, Wyoming, now seems to self-consciously mimic the sets of the old Western movies it once inspired. There is still a very important authenticity here in the West, but some of us have the nagging feeling that in an odd, out-of-body way, we risk imitating what was once a genuine way of life, rather than actually living it. Historian Hal Rothman has said, "The embrace of tourism triggers an all-encompassing contest for the soul of a place."[13] In the complicated, generous process by which the West has shared, sold (or at least rented), and generally celebrated its fly fishing, that contest has muddled our hopes of knowing the genuine.

And yet, at least some of us are sure it is here. We know that authenticity has endured. There *is* such a thing as western fly fishing, and it is in good part the product of a long, distinctive, and flavorful history. Through much of the past two centuries, for example, at least before the great fly-fishing publishing and marketing binge of the past thirty years and before the Web sites and chat rooms and conclaves and clubs and chapters that have appeared more recently, it was possible for a western fly-fishing theorist to operate in a fair amount of isolation. It was, in other words, possible for an angler to be authentically local in approach—to react to the imperatives of his environment, to conduct a long, probing conversation with his river, and then to cook up theories, tackle, or even attitudes that were the robust product of such local impulses and conditions.

My favorite example of this independence is western Montana's long tradition of woven-hair flies, which are in part the subject of chapter 5. This unique subcraft arose in the 1920s and serves as a terrific example of local craft going its own unique, idiosyncratic way. Here, in fact, is something very like a folk art, though its achievements and aesthetics are sadly neglected by regional historians, folklorists, and others who should be interested in such a singular development.

But even in the survival of regionally distinct traditions, there are new complications. It seems pretty certain that during the three decades of my own involvement in the sport of fly fishing, a kind of homogenization has set in, so that even in the remotest corners of the West such quirky genius has less chance to flower than it once did.

Let me give an example of this change. Starting about thirty-five years ago, West Yellowstone fly-fishing writer Charles Brooks published a series of books that codified and promoted what was at the time a distinctly regional style of fly tying and fly fishing. These manuals, which gathered up a lot of local wisdom and practice that already existed, literally rewrote the book on fly fishing around here. Charlie passed away some years ago, but his work is regularly invoked by modern regional fly-fishing writers. Charlie's huge, heavily weighted flies, his almost acrobatic line-controlling techniques, and an assortment of other insights and advice, strained and expanded the sport's theoretical and aesthetic borders for many fishermen. And, in a diffuse but identifiable way, Charlie's approaches became absorbed in the national fishing style. You might not find many of the specific fly patterns that Charlie developed in the regional fly shops today, but you will find mounds of their descendants. And on the streams, you will find many fishermen approaching the water with a somewhat different frame of mind than before Charlie came along. Though he did not do this alone, he was a significant force in causing the change.[14]

But I am almost certain that another Charlie Brooks could not come along now and make such big waves and legitimize so many new things at once. Things have changed that much in just thirty years. Charlie's generation may have been the last one to see any point in keeping the old-fashioned secrets that so many anglers cherished for so many years. The volume of communication among anglers today is stunning. With our current flood of writing and publishing and e-fishing and e-commerce, fly fishers everywhere sound more and more like each other, fish more and more like each other, and find it a lot easier to all know the same things. In such an information-intense community, it's pretty hard to start a revolution.

But there are still local experts and there are still local developments that matter, whether in fly pattern, in fishing technique, in theory, or even in such rarified matters as ethics and spirituality. And most important, fly fishing is still a great source of personal fulfillment, intellectual distraction, and fun. It's just that the greater society of fly fishing is less susceptible to being surprised or changed by what its members hear from any far corner of the sport.

Fly fishing seems to be experiencing the same globalization of community that affects the rest of humanity's activities. I may be vastly annoyed by all the out-of-state plates along my favorite streams, but it wouldn't surprise me in the least to learn that many of those tourist-anglers know the local insect hatches on my streams and are able to catch the local fish better than I ever will. After all, one important reason that I'm any good at catching western trout is the five-summer apprenticeship I served trying to catch the jumpy *eastern* trout in Vermont's notoriously difficult Battenkill. Maybe western fishermen were never as distinct a type as we thought we were, but we are less distinct all the time.

So, though we who live in the West do bring a vast amount of quirky personality, local color, oddball theorizing, and even some occasional class to the western fly-fishing scene, western fly fishing's distinctiveness is lucky that it doesn't have to depend on us. Instead I think it depends upon other even less definable or tangible things. These things have less to do with us, or with the fish, than they do with the river itself.

They have to do, quite necessarily, with these stunning western landscapes. Such sweep and scale aren't unknown in the East, but they aren't everyday things either. Wherever they occur on earth, high places and remote places beckon and enchant us.

There abides in the western fishing scene a fresher sense of a frontier. In some strange way, this western scene can still be

Western fly fishing's distinctiveness is based in good part on the wild landscapes through which the rivers run. The idea of the native wildness of the West is still supported here and there by the presence of such forceful wilderness symbols as the grizzly bear. Whether anglers actually see a bear or its tracks, or just enjoy the awareness of being in grizzly bear habitat, there is a heightened sense of wildness, even of frontier.

Yellowstone National Park, National Park Service

imagined by its inhabitants, local or visitor, as something new, even as something raw. A surprising variety of imagined Wests work in this respect. They work whether the angler perceives this frontier as the backdrop of a sociologically tidy John Wayne movie or as the scene of a painful multicultural drama of conquest and tragedy. There is a special excitement whether the angler looks back on a family history deeply connected to the frontier or just abstractly admires the *idea* of such connections. The presence of grizzly bears, elk, and even wolves near some of these rivers further heightens the sense of something almost primordial encountered during a day's fishing. In Pennsylvania's limestone country, on Long Island's history-rich little streams, or in New England's rugged valleys, we may fish in authentically colonial landscapes, but in the West we fish the Pleistocene. And the more raw and unsettled the landscape we fish, the more heightened our sense of exploration and discovery, the stronger our sense of possibility, and the more profound our hope.[15]

The West, Wallace Stegner's native *home* of such hopes, has inspired just such sentiments in generations of fly fishers. In a place like this, anything seems possible, and fly fishing, like the West itself, is in good part an exercise in imagination, if not dreams.

In the West, we fish in settings so obviously heroic that the heroism might rub off on us. After all, fishermen are heroes in their own little dramas and are secretly involved in a sort of quest that has to do with much more than catching a bigger fish—as much as we do hope for that. In the West, we can sense a newness to the landscape that suggests, even promises, the sort of better world that all fishermen harbor in their hearts as the great hope of being out there in the first place.[16]

And in the West, fly fishing offers us other, greater opportunities. If we stop perceiving fly fishing merely as something people do when they're not doing something significant and recognize it as a window on what matters about the West, the sport may become more than entertainment, distraction, and tourism. Fly fishing as culture has things to teach us, perhaps on a more modest scale than some other subjects, but with its own unique slant. It may even give us one more way to get at greater questions—why, for one thing, the West and its contentious, endlessly reinterpreted history and culture matter so much. And why, for another, the stakes seem so high, in so many ways besides the landing or losing of a trout, along these beautiful western rivers.

The Yellowstone River provided the Washburn Party
with sport and food wherever they encountered it
in the early portions of their journey.

Second Canon, Yellowstone River, from Harry J. Norton,
Wonder-Land Illustrated (Virginia City, Mont.: privately printed), p. 31

CHAPTER THREE

Yellowstone I
Sport, Science, and Subsistence
in 1870

History, to be accurate, must be romantic
as well as scientific.

—William Goetzmann, *Exploration and Empire:*
The Explorer and the Scientist in the Winning
of the American West (1967)

Early in *The Life and Strange Surprising Adventures of*
Robinson Crusoe, of York, Mariner, Written by himself
(1719), Daniel Defoe's shipwrecked hero makes the following diary entry: "May 4. I went a fishing, but caught not one
fish that I durst eat of, till I was weary of my sport; when,
just going to leave off, I caught a young dolphin."[1]

With this one comment, the durable Mr. Crusoe inadvertently suggested the complications we face when we attempt
to categorize fishing as a human endeavor. Here was a man
for whom fishing was an urgent matter of survival, yet it was
also a "sport." To the modern untrained ear, a "sport" is a
pastime—something done at best to relax and invigorate, at
worst just to kill time. To the ear of Daniel Defoe, sport was

apparently something far more complicated than that.

As it still should be. There is a good deal of messiness in the terminology of sport, though it is nothing compared to the casual, offhanded manner in which many writers, including academics whom one would expect to be more careful, reduce such ancient human pursuits as hunting and fishing to superficial trivialities. Sport fishing and sport hunting, at the hands of such writers, are "mere" sport, which is to say they exist only to generate "fun."

The rhetorical blurring of the two terms "sports" and "games" is likewise far advanced and will probably become more confused as American society becomes progressively less comfortable with the traditional "blood sports" (as if ice hockey is not a blood sport). I cannot correct this problem but only point it out to suggest further the imprecision of the language. When most modern Americans say they are discussing "sports," they usually mean "games."

Though not all sports are games, neither are all games sports. Hunting elk is hardly anyone's idea of a game; Monopoly is no one's idea of a sport. And yet, historian John McDonald was right when he aptly said that "a sport or game may be thought of as the set of rules that describes it."[2] The two categories may have more in common than they have in distinction.

The imprecision and carelessness of our terminology in sport is a reflection of the amazing capacity of sport for both durability and flexibility. Part of sport's fascination for us as an institution worthy of study should be the way it is transformed during its long societal career, even to the extent that it can outlive its apparent original cause for existence. For those who believe that sports have tended to arise in good part from utilitarian practice—as rodeo, for example, tests and celebrates skills needed on a working ranch—it might seem counterintuitive that a sport would hang on after people no longer had any use for its skills. But sports can and do transcend at least some of the reasons for their creation. We might even say that over the course of a few generations, one person's sport can eventually become another person's game.

To illustrate the evolution, or at least transformation, of a sport from the realm of the immediately practical to something more esoteric, classics scholar David Sansone used the example of javelin throwing, which is still a vital athletic event despite several centuries having passed since there was a going military need for javelin throwers. We now throw javelins for reasons other than keeping a battlefield skill in shape.[3]

In a literate society in which records are easily kept and invoked, sport is an intergenerational enterprise. Today's javelin thrower has relevance in part because he or she competes with the records of every previous javelin thrower, just as today's fisherman casts in the shadow of countless earlier angling theorists, philosophers, and other temporally remote companions. And, as any determined sports nostalgist will tell you, once a sport has accumulated enough generations of precise statistics, wispy remembrance, and glowing legend, there will be a group of enthusiasts—both fans and actual practitioners—wanting to prop it all up with continued performance of like kind.[4]

In the cases of hunting and fishing, and especially fishing, this urge to perpetuate a sport provides us with a delicious irony. Historian Adrian Bantjes has noted that historians generally have paid no attention to the scholarly opportunities that angling history so generously presents:

> A vast and theoretically sophisticated literature on sports history and leisure has emerged, influenced by the new social history, anthropology, and, most recently, cultural studies. Thus, the theoretical and analytical tools needed to approach the topic, whether from the perspective of class, religion, gender, race, identity, or capitalism, are readily available. . . . Yet, even though an extensive and theoretically sophisticated historiography exists for sports such as baseball and football, angling history remains rather neglected.[5]

Here's the irony. While historians widely ignore the study of these important human activities, the activities themselves thrived and defined themselves in good part through a passionate devotion to their own long traditions. For their enthusiasts, history is an essential part of these sports. These people may not have written very good histories of themselves, but they got little help from professional historians, so who is at fault if the history they now hold dear is, even more than most history, so inclined to ancestor worship and yarn spinning?[6]

Consideration of Robinson Crusoe and javelin throwers may seem a roundabout way to approach the variety of influences and impulses behind fishing in the frontier West. But the parallels between the javelin and the fly rod are perhaps deeper and more numerous than they might appear. The West provides some striking examples of the several ways in which a sport may simultaneously be valued in a given social setting.

SPORT FISHING AND SCIENCE

Historian Daniel Justin Herman, in *Hunting and the American Imagination* (2001), says that an important element of the "new Americanness" of being a proper sportsman in the early-nineteenth-century United States was an interest in natural history. Based on his comparison of the amount of attention spent on natural history and hunting in America's early sporting press, Herman says that by the 1830s, "To be a hunter would henceforth mean to know the secrets of science; indeed, to be a hunter was to unlock the puzzle of nature itself, at least insofar as that could be accomplished by knowing the haunts, habits, and physical characteristics of game animals."[7]

This was not strictly an American development; Herman's description of the rise of the sportsman-naturalist is identical to what is reported for Canada. Historian Karen Wonders, writing similarly about the nineteenth-century Canadian wilderness, has described that nation's experience:

> The sportsman cult was also closely tied to the study of natural history. Sportsmen were the first to write specifically and at length about nature and the pleasures of hunting and fishing in the New

World while adorning their hunting lodges and
fishing huts with paintings and sculptures that captured, so to speak, the passion of their sport.[8]

These statements, which seem to indicate a nineteenth-
century origin for—or increase in—the sport hunter's natural
history enthusiasms, raise an interesting question: Over the past
several centuries, have there been qualitative or quantitative
differences in how the writers of hunting and fishing literature
valued natural history? I raise this question because natural
history as a significant narrative element in books on fishing
was not a product of the nineteenth century. Natural history,
or its earlier equivalents, was a routine and important part
of fishing instructional manuals almost from the first publication of such works, and remained so in many general fishing books in the United States until late in the 1800s.[9]

In the 1800s, as audience size and advances in printing
technology justified more specialization in subject matter in
a given book, proportionately fewer British and American
books on fishing seem to have included in-depth information
on the lives of game fish. But still, books such as Thaddeus
Norris's *American Anglers Book* (1864) and Genio Scott's
Fishing in American Waters (1869) were almost encyclopedic
in their coverage of sport-fish natural history.[10]

By the 1870s, then, even the modestly well-read angler
who considered himself to be a legitimate sportsman was
likely to have an interest in information about his favorite
fish that wasn't directly necessary to catch them. In the years
after the Civil War, sportsmen-naturalists exemplified by

Theodore Roosevelt and George Bird Grinnell among the hunters and by James Henshall and Robert Barnwell Roosevelt among the fishermen would work hard to instill that interest in their fellow outdoor enthusiasts.

And it was a good time to be excited about natural history. In 1870, it was still possible to be both a leading fisheries authority and a leading popular fishing writer; the categories and specializations had not yet hardened and isolated the professionals in those two fields to the extent they have today, when such combinations are rare.[11] In 1870, there were still new sport-fish species being formally "discovered" (though all were long known to Native Americans, and some had been known to Euramericans). It was still an era in which natural history study could be characterized as a genuine adventure, especially in less-known regions of the West. It was still very much possible for a gifted amateur, operating outside the formal realm of academic study, to make an important discovery.

A DISTINGUISHED SET OF ANGLERS

The experiences of the famous Washburn-Langford-Doane Expedition (hereinafter the Washburn Party), who visited the Yellowstone Plateau in the late summer of 1870, serve as a helpful illustration of the complex interplay of sport, subsistence, and science in one of the last large portions of the West that had still not been officially explored.[12]

The Washburn Party has been worth study merely for the distinction of its members. Their elected commander was Henry Dana Washburn, a former Civil War general and Indiana

Nathaniel Langford, a member of the Washburn Party and a prominent advocate for the creation of Yellowstone National Park, became the park's first superintendent less than two years after the expedition.

Yellowstone National Park, National Park Service

congressman, now Surveyor General of Montana Territory. The party of nineteen included, among others, Helena judge Cornelius Hedges, Montana Territorial Assistant Assessor of Internal Revenue Walter Trumbull (son of Illinois U.S. senator Lyman Trumbull), banker-businessman Samuel Hauser, and former Montana Territory Collector of Internal Revenue Nathaniel Langford (who, in one of those complex maneuverings so belovedly characteristic of territorial politics, had recently come as close as possible to being appointed Montana territorial governor without actually occupying the office). Their small military escort was under the command of Lieutenant Gustavus Doane, who would write the most authoritative account of the trip.[13]

What may have most distinguished this already distinguished group as explorers, however, was their exceptional literary output following the expedition. They had a finely tuned and quite accurate sense of the historical significance of what they were doing, and they left historians a wonderful treasury of first-hand accounts and impressions, many of which were published in newspapers and magazines in the months following the trip. This wealth of material has been employed by historians and others to better understand the 1870s view of wild nature, the rise of the national park idea, Native American activities in and effects on the Yellowstone region, historic wildlife populations and distribution, and other elements of the Yellowstone setting in 1870. The literary legacy of the Washburn Party has only grown in value over the years.

Johan Huizinga, in *Homo Ludens: A Study of the Play*

Element in Human Culture (1950), said that "It is ancient wisdom, but it is also a little cheap, to call all human activity 'play.'" For Huizinga, "play is to be understood here not as a biological phenomenon but as a cultural phenomenon."[14] The Washburn Party's trout-fishing experiences illustrate the depth and variety of that cultural phenomenon. By taking their trout-fishing tools, practices, and values into a wilderness setting, the Washburn Party offer us a rewarding glimpse of how complicated a thing it is for a person to toss a hook and line into a river.

Sportsmen on the Trail

The area that was to become Yellowstone National Park in 1872 was by no means unexplored in 1870. Not only had Native Americans been intimately familiar with this landscape for thousands of years, but also whites had been visiting it for more than six decades. The Washburn Party saw signs of a number of previous white visitors on their trip, and twice while in the present park area they encountered other whites.

But the many accounts of the wonders of Yellowstone provided by trappers, prospectors, and other early white visitors had not constituted a respected or widely accepted body of knowledge. So, in a vividly real social sense, the Washburn Party, like a few of Yellowstone's other early "exploration" parties, actually was engaging in a kind of formal discovery.[15]

Washburn Party members, having traveled from Helena to Bozeman between August 17 and August 20, were joined by Lieutenant Doane and his small detachment of five soldiers at Fort Ellis, just east of Bozeman. The group set out on

*Lieutenant Gustavus Doane commanded the small military escort
of the Washburn Party. His superb official report on the Washburn
Expedition contained the best natural history account
of Yellowstone's cutthroat trout published to that date.*

Yellowstone National Park, National Park Service

August 22 and straggled across the landscape of the upper Yellowstone region for several weeks before returning home by way of the Madison Valley.

Many of the members of the party were sportsmen, and hunting and fishing were obvious attractions of this trip. Trumbull no doubt expressed the anticipation that several of them felt when he wrote that "We intended to hunt for all sorts of large game, Indians only excepted. No one desired to find any of them."[16] (I will leave Trumbull's eyebrow-raising equating of Native Americans with "large game" for another time, or another historian; as I said, this material continues to surprise and challenge us.)

That first night on the trail, camped along Trail Creek, Hedges wrote in his diary, perhaps with a little competitive triumph, that he "Caught the first trout."[17] Trumbull added, in somewhat grumpy detail, that "some of the party fished with very limited success, catching only about half a dozen fish by their united and untiring efforts."[18]

The group's various members fished frequently from then on, until they left the region that would soon become Yellowstone Park. Fishing-minded readers would enjoy reading their many mentions of the trout, but here we will confine ourselves to especially telling episodes.

On August 23, they were in what is now known as Paradise Valley, the famously picturesque stretch of the Yellowstone River Valley south of Livingston. They stopped at the Bottler Ranch, near present Emigrant, and camped near this pioneer holding that was known as the last outpost of civilization north of the Yellowstone Plateau. Hedges said, "I

*Cornelius Hedges, a graduate of Harvard Law School
and later a Montana judge, was among the most
enthusiastic anglers in the Washburn Party.*

Montana Historical Society Photograph Archives, Helena

went down to fish after camping. had no bate but meat
which they wouldnt touch."[19]

Here Hedges introduces us to a key element in the society
of angling: the rivalries among anglers. Bait fishing was, even
then, seen as the least cosmopolitan form of fishing.
According to the loftiest dictates of refined sporting society,
gentlemen (or snobs, depending upon your perspective) pre-

ferred sophisticated tackle employing artificial lures or flies. Washburn Party members revealed various opinions about the preference of Yellowstone trout for bait or artificial lures, but when it came to what method caught the most fish, most party members sided with the bait fishermen. In this case, though, Hedges's implication is a bit unclear. He could have meant that he needed more sophisticated tackle, such as fly-fishing gear, or he could just have been pointing up the inferiority of meat (presumably beef, elk, or other game) to grasshoppers, which were the most acclaimed and successful bait of the entire trip. Judging from his later experiences, the latter was the more likely case.

On August 24, Hedges said, "just before camping we crossed a good sized creek with big boulders & recent signs of bear among the cherry bushes. Our advance had a jack rabbit & sage hen but no fish. couldn't catch any grasshoppers. couldnt get any pole but caught some fish with [Benjamin] Stickney's pole."[20] These remarks reveal what may well have been a common practice among the fishermen, at least among those not using store-bought tackle. As already noted, Hedges previously fished on August 22, so he must have had a "pole" that day. Because poles were so readily had at streamside, fishermen might not have bothered to carry one with them or on the pack animals. At the end of a day's fishing, they could just discard the pole, wind their line around something convenient (like a very short stick), and stow it away until needed again. The risk of this approach, as Hedges appears to have been noting on August 24, was in not finding a suitable pole the next time.

Also on August 24, Langford said that "During the forenoon some of the escort were very successful fishing for trout."[21] This is our first indication that the soldiers under Lieutenant Doane were also fishing and that they were often quite successful. Doane echoed Langford's sentiment, saying that "Our mess-table was here supplied with antelope, hare, ducks, and grouse killed during the day, with fish caught *ad libitum* in the afternoon."[22] Fish were already assuming a primary nutritional role for the party—a role that would increase in significance as the trip continued.

SPORTSMEN-NATURALISTS

Near Yankee Jim Canyon, Trumbull made the first fish-related natural history observations. He said, "During the day plenty of small game was killed, and the fishing was found to be excellent. Trout and white-fish were abundant—and such trout! They can only be found in the neighborhood of the Rocky Mountains, and on the Pacific Slope. Few of them weighed less than two pounds, and many were over three. They had not been educated up to the fly; but when their attention was respectfully solicited to a transfixed grasshopper, they seldom failed to respond."[23]

Here again, sporting values intrude on the narrative we are reconstructing. Trumbull was operating in an established literary convention with his remark about the trout not being educated "up to the fly." The suggestion that North American trout lacked the polish to respond to high-quality tackle was an occasional item of angling humor and at times seemed even to imply a certain pride, that our trout were not snobs.[24]

Again, bait was the preferred choice of the angler, but now we know that flies were tried by at least one party member.

As we will see later in this book, this is hardly the only time when the tackle that was supposedly the most refined did not work or was not as effective as less sophisticated gear. The theme of trout not taking costly and presumably well-designed flies is an interesting one because of what it says about anglers more than for what it says about trout. Experienced anglers who have encountered little-fished-for backcountry trout know that they will sometimes find them as unresponsive as hard-fished roadside trout. Exactly why such apparently naive fish should be reluctant to take a fly no doubt has to do with the natural foods they are enjoying right then, the artificial flies being presented to them, the skill of the anglers, and other imponderables. I don't find a great mystery in the occasional account of wilderness trout refusing to feed on the best artificial flies and lures. It has happened to me and my friends too often to be novel and has just reinforced the old wisdom, "That's why they call it 'going fishing' instead of 'going catching.'"

Of equal interest is Trumbull's mention of whitefish. Whitefish were native to the Yellowstone River through its entire length as far upstream as Knowles Falls, in present northern Yellowstone Park. They were also native to the Madison River drainage, by which route the party left the park area and returned to Bozeman. Presumably they were sometimes part of the party's catch, but this is the only mention any party member would make of them. As the "poor sisters" of trout in the prevailing sport fisher's view (then as now), whitefish were rarely worth bragging about.

Also in his August 24 entry, Doane (writing in a report that was no doubt polished and revised after the trip) first discussed the dependability of fish as a supplemental food source for the party when he said that "Several of the party were very successful during the morning in fishing for trout, of which we afterward had an abundant and continued supply."[25]

Doane here also made his first contribution to the natural history of the fish: "The Yellowstone trout are peculiar, being the largest of the genus caught in waters flowing east. Their numbers are perfectly fabulous, but their appetites extremely dainty. One may fish with the finest tackle of eastern sportsmen, when the water appears to be alive with them, all day long without a bite. Grasshoppers are their peculiar weakness, and using them for a bait the most awkward angler can fill a champagne-basket in an hour or two. They do not bite with the spiteful greediness of eastern brook trout, but amount to much more in the way of subsistence when caught. Their flesh is of a bright yellow color on the inside of the body, and of a flavor unsurpassed."[26]

Doane, in his remark about the Yellowstone cutthroat trout being "the largest of the genus caught in waters flowing east," seems to have been comparing the Yellowstone cutthroat with trout in the Missouri River (or its source rivers, the Gallatin, Madison, and Jefferson) or any of the many other rivers that join the Missouri and host trout populations. Either he had, or he had learned from someone with, personal acquaintance with the various trout populations east of the Continental Divide. It is an interesting observation, but not one that seems supported by the historical record; early records of Missouri River trout, dating back as far as Lewis and Clark's travels up and down the river in 1805–1806, suggest that Missouri River trout were sizeable.

Doane's comments on the behavior of the eastern brook trout were possibly based on second-hand information, perhaps from another member of the party; Doane himself spent very little time in the East in his life.[27] It would be nice to know if his later experiences with Yellowstone cutthroats on this trip changed his mind, but he did not return to the subject in later journal entries. Small cutthroat trout in upland freestone streams seem to feed at least as hastily and vigorously as do eastern brook trout (which have, regrettably, displaced them from many of their native waters in the West).

On August 25, the party continued on an apparent Indian trail through Yankee Jim Canyon, just a few miles north of what would become Yellowstone Park. At some point during the day, party member Warren Gillette "Tried my luck at fishing in Y.S.—caught nothing. others of the party caught some fine fish—had for supper last night & breakfast this a.m. Antelope, Rabbit, Grouse, duck & fish."[28] As we will see, Gillette was one of the party who carried fly-fishing gear. Perhaps his lack of success was the inspiration for Doane's remark about "the finest tackle of eastern sportsmen" not serving well.

The party followed the Yellowstone River drainage upstream, finding plenty of fish and other game. On August 28, Gillette, now in the area that would become Yellowstone Park and fishing the Yellowstone River near the mouth of

Warren Gillette, perhaps the most accomplished outdoorsman in the Washburn Party, was the first person known to have fly fished in what would become Yellowstone Park.

Montana Historical Society Photograph Archives, Helena

Tower Creek, "Caught 7 fine trout that would weigh from 2 to 2-1/2 pounds each. These fish are not gamy like the trout in the east. They make but little resistance in being taken from the water & do not run with the hook after taking the bait."[29] Gillette was a native of New York, where he lived until attending Oberlin College in Ohio. His background and his comments this day further lead to the conclusion that he, at least, was using "eastern" tackle and was familiar with the native eastern brook trout.

It is part of the Yellowstone cutthroat's mixed reputation among modern fly fishers that it is, indeed, not as "gamy" as some other species of trout. The prevailing opinion is that, of the common trout species, Yellowstone cutthroats are the least strong fighters when hooked. For example, unlike their near cousins the rainbows, Yellowstone cutthroats rarely jump when hooked.[30] But many of today's trout fishermen, more than a century further along in the sport's ethical development, do not place quite as high a premium on the "fight" as did earlier generations of anglers. Especially those anglers who practice catch-and-release seek to land the fish as quickly as possible, because the fish's struggle to escape— once such a prized part of the fishing experience—can exhaust it beyond recovery.

SPORTSMEN-SURVIVALISTS

September arrived as the party enjoyed the scenery, fishing, and hunting around the Grand Canyon of the Yellowstone. Langford worried about the lateness of the season and the prospects for provisions: "However, the perceptible decline in our larder, and the uncertainty of the time to be occupied in further exploration, forbid more than two days' stay at the falls and cañon."[31] The party would display a growing sense of urgency to keep moving, despite all their enthusiasm for discovery and wonder.

There was another risk. There were many elk and other large animals in Yellowstone, in appropriate habitats. But those habitats were not uniformly distributed across the landscape, nor was the wildlife necessarily handy when hunters wanted food. And if the animals should begin to migrate to winter ranges in lower country far from the party's travel route, that source of meat would disappear. Only some birds and the trout would remain.

At Yellowstone Lake that first week of September, Washburn joined the chorus of angling theorists who seemed to believe, or at least joked, that wild trout have to be taught to take flies: "The fishing, which had been good all the way up the river, proved remarkably so in the lake. Trout from 2 to 4 pounds were to be had for the taking. Flies proved useless, as the fish had not been educated up to that point."[32] He did not specify who, precisely, was fishing with flies, but this is probably the earliest known reference to the use of flies in what would become Yellowstone Park.

Like anglers of all generations, the Washburn Party enlisted a satisfying array of excuses to explain those days when they didn't catch much, including lousy tackle, bad weather, poor bait, heavy streamside brush, and ignorant fish (blaming the fish is always an especially entertaining rationalization). Unlike most modern anglers, however, party

In 1871, the year after the Washburn Party traveled past the same spot, the pioneering western photographer William Henry Jackson photographed the southeast arm of Yellowstone Lake where the upper Yellowstone River flows from its delta into the lake.

U.S. Geological Survey

members also listed the threat of physical violence as an interfering factor. At least once, the imagined or real approach of Indians caused anglers to return to camp.[33]

In his September 4 report entry, Doane offered the most extended observation on the characteristics of trout of Yellowstone Lake made by the party:

> Its waters abound with trout to such an extent that the fish at this season are in poor condition, for want of food. No other fish are seen; no minnows, and no small trout. There are also no clams, crabs,

or turtles—nothing but full-grown trout. These could by caught in mule-loads by wading out a few feet in the open waters at any point with a grasshopper bait. Two men could catch them faster than half a dozen could clean and get them ready for the frying pan. Caught in the open lake, their flesh was yellow; but in bays, where the water was strongly impregnated with chemicals, it was blood-red. Many of them were full of long white worms, woven across the interior of the body, and through to the skin on either side. These did not appear to materially affect the condition of the fish, which were apparently as active as the others.[34]

The ambitious Doane, whose duties were limited to accompanying and protecting the party, made good use of the opportunity to distinguish himself as an official explorer, producing the party's most competent and fully documented report, including such formalities as daily temperatures, barometric readings, and elevations. His report was a model of the type, and when it appeared in June 1871, it enjoyed a brief reign as the foremost published scientific source on the wonders of Yellowstone. But even as it appeared, Ferdinand Hayden of the U.S. Geological Survey and Captain John Barlow, an engineer with the U.S. Army's Division of Missouri, were preparing much more professional survey parties (including sportsmen-explorers of their own) that within a year would simply flood the world with scientific information on Yellowstone.

Still, Doane's report remains a literary and informational classic from this early period, and his accounts of the life history of Yellowstone trout were a legitimate contribution to knowledge at the time. Though some of his natural history was suspect (such as the fish lacking food—how had the trout population persisted for thousands of years if there was so little food?—and such as the explanation of the color of the flesh of the trout, which is primarily the result of diet), other parts were astute. Immature Yellowstone cutthroat trout are, indeed, rarely seen; they tend to live in deeper water, out of reach of sport anglers. And the observation of the worms was to be echoed by countless later writers who encountered this visually disturbing but relatively benign (at least to humans) parasite. Doane did not formally identify this creature, but his accurate account of it and its effect on trout preceded by two years Dr. Joseph Leidy's formal description of the tapeworm *Diphyllobothrium*.[35]

Langford, whose reputation as a regional booster is well known by historians, said, in an article in *Scribner's Monthly*, that the lake "is filled with trout, some of gigantic size and peculiar delicacy."[36] There is no evidence in the historical, archaeological, or biological record that the trout of Yellowstone Lake ever achieved "gigantic" size. A twenty-four-inch specimen would be extraordinary, but in the lexicon of anglers of that day even a fish that large would hardly be considered gigantic. It is possible that Langford's own experiences up to that time had involved only smaller trout and by comparison the fish of Yellowstone Lake seemed huge, but it is also possible that describing the trout this way was for Langford just another means of further enhancing his description of the region's glories (and I will admit that a twenty-four-inch trout would meet my personal and much less demanding definition of gigantic).

Hedges, in a newspaper article he later wrote about Yellowstone Lake, gave us the party's best single reminiscence of what Yellowstone Lake angling was like for a true enthusiast. This account stands as by far the most extended and meaningful personal sport-fishing narrative to that point in the Yellowstone area's literary history.

> My individual taste led me to fishing, and I venture that none of the party dare complain that they did not have all the fine trout that their several appetites and capacities could provide storage for. Indeed, I feel in gratitude bound to bear testimony that for fine fish, and solid, satisfying fun, there is no body of water under the sun more attractive to the ambitious fisherman than the Yellowstone Lake. While upon the subject of fishing, allow me to relate one or two instances of personal experience. One day, after the loss of our comrade [later in September], and when rations were getting short, I was deputed to lay in a stock of fish to eke our scanty larder on our homeward journey. Proud of this tribute to my piscatory skill, I endeavored under some difficulties, to justify the expectations of my companions, and in about two hours, while the waves were comparatively quiet, I strewed the beach with about 50

Visitors to Yellowstone Park in its early days were fond of cooking freshly caught live trout in lakeside hot springs. Many enjoyed the novelty of cooking the trout without removing it from the hook, merely swinging the just-caught fish from the cold water of the lake into a nearby hot spring. Washburn Party member Cornelius Hedges, however, reacted with commendable horror when he accidentally dunked and boiled a trout in a hot spring.

From William Cullen Bryant, ed., *Picturesque America,*
or the Land We Live In, 2 vols. (New York: D. Appleton, 1872), 1:309

beauties, not one of which would weigh less than 2 pounds, while the average weight was about 3 pounds. Another incident, illustrative of the proximity of hot springs rather than of trouting: Near the southwest corner of the lake is a large basin of exceedingly hot springs. These springs cover a large field. Some are in the very margin of the lake, while others rise under the lake and indicate their locality by steam and ebullition upon the lake's surface when the waves are not too uneasy. One spring of large size, unfathomable depth, sending out a continuous stream of at least 50 inches of scalding water, is still separated from the cool water of the lake by a rocky partition, not more than a foot thick in places. I returned along the narrow rim of this partition, and catching sight of some expectant trout lying in easy reach, I solicited their attention to a transfixed grasshopper, and meeting an early and energetic response, I attempted to land my prize beyond the spring, but unfortunately for the fish, he escaped the hook to plunge into this boiling spring. As soon as possible I relieved the agonized creature by throwing him out with my pole, and though his contortions were not fully ended, his skin came off and he had all the appearance of being boiled through. The incident, though excusable as an incident, was too shocking to repeat.

We noted it as a singular fact that we saw no other fish than trout in the lake, and no small fish of any sort. There was a wide contrast in the color of the meat of these trout. While most of them were as richly red as salmon, others were quite white; and as a frank confession is good for the soul, we will relieve our own by confessing that some at our very last camp on the lake were found to be wormy.[37]

Despite Hedges's obvious horror at causing such agony to the fish that was accidentally boiled, it was apparently not true that it was "too shocking to repeat." In fact he was anticipating a long-popular (if ghastly) practice among Yellowstone vacationers. Purposely cooking live fish in several hot springs near good fishing waters became a popular visitor attraction in Yellowstone for many years after the park was established. The practice was not made illegal until 1929.

As the party traveled the forested country around Yellowstone Lake, Langford's concerns about food were realized. The easy hunting was past, and their other provisions ran low. On September 6, Hedges said, "Had nothing but salt meat today. Poorest camp we have had in tangled woods."[38] But on September 7, now near the southern end of the Southeast Arm of Yellowstone Lake, Hedges said, "I went out and had much fun catching trout. got about a doz & had a good supper."[39]

On September 9, disaster struck. As the party thrashed through the heavy downfall of timber south of the lake, fifty-four-year-old Truman Everts became separated from the group, and despite the heroic efforts of party members who searched for him even after the first snowfalls, he wandered lost for thirty-seven days, finally being rescued by two local mountaineers in the northern part of the present park. Some of his most exasperating experiences in trying to feed himself in the wild involved his attempts to catch fish.[40]

Meanwhile, for the main party, trout were becoming more important as food. On September 10, in camp on Flat Mountain Arm on the southwest shore of Yellowstone Lake, Doane reported that "In the evening large numbers of fish were caught, Private Williamson catching fifty-two large trout,

Nathaniel Langford's map of Yellowstone Lake, though a somewhat misshapen representation of the lake's actual outline, shows the relative locations of the Washburn Party's campsites on that portion of their journey.

From Nathaniel Pitt Langford, *Diary of the Washburn Expedition to the Yellowstone and Firehole Rivers* (n.p.: privately printed, 1905), p. 64

all that two men could carry, in less than an hour."[41] On September 11, Hedges said, "Though it was Sun we wanted fish so much that I went down & caught about a dozen. . . . I am to stay & lay in store of fish."[42] On September 12, Langford said, "During the absence of Washburn and myself Mr. Hedges has spent the day in fishing, catching forty of the fine trout with which the lake abounds. Mr. [Benjamin]

Stickney has to-day made an inventory of our larder, and we find that our luxuries, such as coffee, sugar and flour, are nearly used up, and that we have barely enough of necessary provisions—salt, pepper, etc., to last us ten days longer with economy in their use. We will remain at the lake probably three or four days longer with the hope of finding some trace of Everts, when it will be necessary to turn our faces homewards to avoid general disaster, and in the meantime we will dry a few hundred pounds of trout, and carry them with us as a precautionary measure against starvation."[43]

On September 16, Doane reported the party's preparations to leave the lake: "We spent the evening in collecting specimens

Washburn Party members encountered the Firehole River when that now famous trout stream was still fishless, cut off from native trout populations downstream in the Madison River drainage by an impassable waterfall. Fan Geyser, Upper Fire Hole Basin, *shows the river and hot-pot landscape they traveled through.*

From Ferdinand V. Hayden, *Twelfth Annual Report of the U.S. Geological and Geophysical Survey of Territory of Wyoming and Idaho, 1878*, Part II (Washington, D.C.: U.S. Government Printing Office, 1883), plate 15 from the different springs and laying in a supply of fish for future use."[44] Hedges added that "I spent most of the time in fishing. caught about 20. didn't have a good pole and didn't want to wade in. Enjoyed the day very much in spite of wet feet and head ache."[45] As on several other occasions, we find here a report that subsistence fishing was also sport fishing; he fished for meat, but he still had fun.

On September 17, the main party moved west toward the headwaters of the Madison River, which they would follow downstream. On September 18, they emerged from the forest into the Upper Geyser Basin, where they spent a hectic day seeing what they could in this astonishing area. Then they hurried down the Firehole River, which at that time was barren of fish life almost its entire length. On September 19, Hedges said, "No fish in river. Grub getting very thin."[46] That same day, the day before they left the present park area, Langford said, "we are now on short rations, but the fish we dried while camped on Yellowstone lake are doing good service."[47]

Yellowstone's First Fly Fisher?

Warren Gillette and his soldier companions, who had stayed behind at Yellowstone Lake, had no luck finding Everts.[48] They then followed the route of the rest of the party, and on their way they gave us our first specific reference to a known individual fly fishing in what would become Yellowstone Park, one of the world's great fly-fishing destinations. On September 24, Gillette, now on the lower Firehole or upper Madison River, perhaps near the junction of the Firehole and Gibbon Rivers, said, "Tried fishing. My only fly was taken off and could get no bites from meat bait."[49]

For historians of western fly fishing, this is a tantalizing but frustrating statement. Though there were vague and sarcastic comments about fancy tackle, noted earlier, this was the first specific mention of a named individual using a fly on the trip. So it raises questions. Had Gillette just lost his *last* fly—meaning he had lost the others while fishing earlier in the trip? Or had he left his fly book behind in camp and just lost the only fly he had with him? Had he lost the fly in a fish, an underwater snag, a bush? What kind of "meat bait" did he try? Had the advancing season eliminated the option of using grasshoppers? We can only guess, but again, it seems most probable, if not certain, that Gillette was the person who kept trying the "eastern tackle" mentioned by the others and that despite their sarcasms, he found flies more effective or at least more satisfying to use than meat bait. More than that we cannot know without additional evidence.

Eminence for this minor but enviable sporting distinction is entirely in our minds, rather than in theirs. Knowing what Yellowstone was to become as a fly fisher's "Mecca," we cannot help enjoying vicariously getting there first, and valuing that experience quite highly.

But the distinction seems to have been minor, if noticed at all, among these 1870s anglers. Certainly at that time, when Yellowstone's fabulous later aura as an angling paradise was little more than a glimmer in the eyes of a few promoters of railroad tourism, Gillette and his companions would not have been likely to place much significance on being the original fly fisher in Yellowstone Park, which did not even exist yet. They had no reason to differentiate the area now within the boundaries of the park from all the other lands they crossed.

Also, the social separation of "types" of fishermen was probably not as advanced as it would be in only a few decades. Fly fishers had prided themselves as being the highest class and most sophisticated of anglers long before the first recorded references to fly fishing in North America in the late 1700s. Obviously, members of the Washburn Party enjoyed ridiculing fancy eastern tackle; they were aware of prevailing hierarchies. But many American trout fishermen of the mid-1800s, even if they were aware of the social stratification involved in using different kinds of tackle, were still probably generalists who fished in a variety of ways, as the situation demanded. If they could afford fly-fishing tackle, fly fishing was one method they employed. But even in 1870, I suspect that most of these anglers were likely to identify or define themselves primarily as *trout* fishermen (that is, in terms of the species of fish they sought) rather than as *fly* fishers (that is, in terms of the tackle they used).[50] Thus, being the first fly fisher would have meant little, or at least much less, to them than it does to us now.

Conclusions

We might divide the historical interest of the Washburn Party's fish-related exploits into two areas. The first is in the field of sport history. Here they left us a vivid account of fishing what hyperbolic outdoor writers would call "virgin waters." Though untold generations of native people and any number of earlier white visitors had presumably caught trout in Yellowstone, the Washburn Party left us the first reasonably detailed account of it, thus serving as pioneer sporting journalists in this now world-famous fishing destination. They used a variety of tackle, from the most basic to the most sophisticated, but they left us all too little information on such matters as tackle and line specifications, fly patterns, and other details of interest to angling antiquarians.

They displayed an awareness of competing sporting styles and codes of their time by their sarcastic comments about the "finest tackle of eastern sportsmen," comments which, it seems likely, also implied a certain pride in their frontier competence at not needing such effete fripperies. Their values were otherwise not surprising for their times, except perhaps in Hedge's sympathetic portrayal of the agony of a fish he accidentally dunked in a hot spring. They were typical of their time in killing very large numbers of fish, but deserve pardon from the critical judgments of later generations for these apparent excesses because they were counting on the fish for survival and evidently consumed most or all of the fish they caught. Even Private Williamson's huge catch of fifty-two trout on September 10 must be kept in perspective by calculating how little time such a haul would last when confronted by the appetites of nineteen hungry travelers.

Perhaps the most important part of their sport-fishing literary legacy was simply in showing the modern angler what is at stake in managing wild trout fisheries. The first literate sportsmen into a new region provide us with a kind of baseline of fish and game conditions against which we can measure all later attempts to sustain and protect these resources. Before the near-catastrophic problems of the past ten years, when both illegally introduced lake trout and the spread of whirling disease have taken a heavy toll on the trout of Yellowstone Lake, modern management had in fact restored the fish population from terrible overfishing in the 1950s and 1960s to something nearly resembling the rapturous descriptions of the Washburn Party. In today's crowded angling world, that was a great achievement, and it now stands as a fine goal for managers attempting to restore the trout of Yellowstone Lake again.

The second area of interest is a hodgepodge of impressions that the Washburn Party provides other historical specialists. To the historian of western natural history, they provided some modest but meaningful first-hand observations on the region's trout—nothing on the scale of their lengthy accounts of the geography and geothermal wonders, but still information new to biologists.

To the historian of western exploration, trout should, but do not, loom large in this particular chapter of the "discovery" of the West, if only because without trout in those critical mid-September days, the Washburn Party would have been in serious trouble.

To historians of the development and eventual solidification of the national park idea as embodied in the Yellowstone Park Act of March 1, 1872, the men's comments on the quality of the fishing are an indication of yet another of the many reasons that could be enlisted by promoters and other pro-park factions in marketing the park to tourists.

The Washburn Party found good fishing near Tower Creek's junction with the Yellowstone River. Rock Pinnacles above Tower Falls *was one of several drawings that appeared in Langford's* Scribner's Monthly *article (May 1871, p. 9). It was based on artwork by Thomas Moran, who would visit Yellowstone's remarkable landscapes with the Hayden Survey in the summer of 1871.*

To historians of western narratives, the trout should matter as the most important wild animal in the history of the Washburn Party. Cumulatively, party members wrote substantially more words about the Yellowstone cutthroat trout than they wrote about any other species.[51] Fishing was, for this or that subset of the party, a means of acquiring food, of testing one's angling skill, of engaging in friendly competition with other sportsmen, and of studying the natural world. Trout were appreciated as food, as sporting quarry, as affirmation or rejection of sporting codes, as scientific objects, and even as potential promotional devices.

Though entranced by the setting, the Washburn Party hesitated to linger more than two days near these falls in the Grand Canyon of the Yellowstone. Scribner's Monthly *titled the scene* Lower Falls of the Yellowstone River, Wyoming: (350 feet in height) *in the May 1871 article (p. 12). The expedition incorrectly estimated the drop of the falls, which is actually 308 feet.*

I don't mean to suggest, based on this analysis, that we must rewrite western history with trout in the middle. I only suggest that trout have, now and then, here and there, been seriously underrated as part of the story.

It would be unfair, for example, to liken the intensity of interest that the Washburn Party displayed in trout to any similar interest shown by other white residents of Montana Territory in their day-to-day lives. Only some people fished, and only some of them depended on fish for food. The average angler in the northern Rocky Mountains in 1870 would have routinely combined sport and subsistence as the only reasons for fishing.

On the other hand, that same average person would have little day-to-day use for all the rich, diverse elements and values of literature, fine arts, music, or any other central human pursuit. Surely one lesson of this analysis of the Washburn Party's fishing is not that we must elevate fishing to a primary focus among historians of the West, but that we should be alert to the opportunities that trout fishing, in its own quiet and unique way, provides us for improving our understanding of all the subtle and unspoken things that our ancestors were up to when they traveled through trout country.

THE FALLACY OF SEPARABILITY

I am grateful to the trout-fishing writings of the Washburn Party because they finally forced from me an admission of complicity in an old and foolish dialogue that should have been disciplined and redirected long ago.

I suppose it is out of habit, or the shortage of obvious alternative approaches, that when we talk about the various kinds of fishing, we act as if the fishing we do for sport, science, or subsistence really are distinct things—as if there can be an unadulterated form of sport fishing and another of subsistence fishing, or that the scientist collecting trout for study might not enjoy the process of catching them (or frying up a specimen or two later). We know it's never that simple, but we still treat it that way all the time—in our scholarly analyses, in our laws, and in our casual conversations. We seem to have little choice.

Probably the most persistent foisters of this particular error on the public perception of fishing are those people who fall into arguments over the morality of fishing. For example, I have often read or heard some indignant soul announce that fishing for sport is morally indefensible, but fishing for subsistence is fine. Another equally indignant soul might say that trophy fishing is the highest and ultimately most rewarding form of fishing, in some sense more valuable even than subsistence fishing.[52]

Tidy assertions like these leave a world of hopeless but helpful questions unanswered. Just for the exercise, I will ask some of them here, not to argue for any position, but to suggest how short a distance we have yet traveled in these and related inquiries.

Claiming that sport will not or should not figure in the catching of a fish to eat is one of the most intriguing components of modern dialogues on the morality of sport fishing. The troublesome nature of such claims might be best illustrated by questions. If it is morally acceptable for me to catch and eat fish, and if I promise to stop fishing as soon as I have caught enough fish to meet my subsistence needs, is it all right for me to go ahead and find personal enrichment (code word for sport) in the process? Does this kind of fishing actually redefine sport simply as the satisfaction one receives from successful subsistence fishing? Or is that satisfaction morally superior to the less savory joys of sport in some way and deserving of a different name?

Or should there be no joy of any kind in the catching of the fish? Must I always discipline myself to shift my soul into moral neutral and harvest fish in the most emotionless way possible, like they were rutabagas?

And if I may not engage in sport while catching fish, does it then cease to matter how I catch them? Shouldn't I just resort to all those brutally efficient alternatives that society has so laboriously weeded out of the sportsman's code during the past few centuries—poisons, guns, traps, nets, explosives—in the interest not only of a more efficient harvest of food, but also to avoid any risk of my inadvertently backsliding into sport by using my rod and reel? After all, if eating the fish makes it okay to kill it, shouldn't I strive to kill it in the way that is least distressing to the fish? It's over pretty quickly with dynamite, you know. It must be an easier death if you're a fish. There's none of this frantic running around with hook and line in your mouth, cranking up your metabolism and exhausting yourself for a while, then being hauled out of the water for photography and execution. With dynamite, there's just a terrific concussion that stuns you or kills your outright, and it's over.

Then there is the issue of the internal complications within each type of fishing, which suggest to me that each has its own qualitative spectrum. Thinking of sport fishing in this way, for example, we might wonder if it is more sporting to use the finest leader and the smallest fly, as was once regarded in some circles as the highest proof of one's skill, or to use heavier tackle that allows us to land the fish more quickly and thus reduce the length of time it suffers (or thus allow ourselves to release it with a better chance of its survival)?

Thinking of subsistence fishing as having its own qualitative spectrum, we might ask if we can judge the relative quality of competing forms of subsistence—for example, on the one hand, the wealthy fly fisher whose just-caught trout is being picturesquely grilled for his lunch by his guide along the river, compared, on the other hand, to the hard-luck bait fisherman ten miles downstream who just landed a couple three-pounders for the family dinner. Both are going to eat the fish they just caught, but I'd vote for the bait-man as most purely fishing for subsistence. But even subsistence isn't a simple idea in the long written history of fishing, and there is reason to doubt that urgency of need is the only criteria by which to measure the "purity" of subsistence fishing. Ever since the publication of the *Treatise of Fishing with an Angle* (1496), anglers have been reminded that sport fishing is a supremely healthy thing for them to do, advantageous to the body and the soul, whether they catch anything or not. The whole point of sport fishing, according to some of our most venerated experts and prophets, is to live on a higher emotional, physical, and spiritual plane. Surely any fully up-to-date holistic assessment of subsistence fishing would have to take into account these significant if non-nutritional benefits of sport fishing. They certainly seem to figure prominently in most defenses of catch-and-release fishing, in which nutritional subsistence is never the point anyway.[53]

Such matters just add to the messiness of fishing's realities. The bait fisherman may be back tomorrow, further depleting the river's population of brood fish. The rich fly fisher may have to emotionally "subsist" on the memory of that one trout lunch for a whole year in his city before he gets a chance to come back and seek fresh subsistence in another fish. Whether we like or dislike these individuals, we had best admit that their lives are complicated.

As for science, its spectrum is pretty murky too. Practically all of those nineteenth-century sportsmen who became natural-history enthusiasts were dilletantes and hobbyists. They contributed nothing to the formal science of fish and game. But is that the point? If we pay intense, admiring attention to the fish we catch, and thereby heighten our knowledge and affection for its world, is peer-reviewed publication also necessary? I'm amazed at some of the astute natural history observations I've heard or read, made by fishermen just because they were well tuned to what was going on in the river. They made those observations cumulatively, building their awareness and perceptual skills day by day, fish by fish, discovery by discovery, often over several decades of watching, and thinking, and fishing (and, by the way, if asked, they wouldn't say they were doing science; they would say they were just doing sport really well).

Last in this parade of tentatives and irresolvables, sport, science, and subsistence certainly aren't the only reasons for fishing. I have several artist friends who turn their catch into poetry, photographs, music, prose, sculpture, or paintings. Is there to be a dispensation for their aesthetic categories?[54]

In short, how many continua are operating parallel to one another when we go fishing, providing this fisherman a little more sport, and that fisherman a little more subsistence, and this other who knows what subtle gift?

All these hypothetical questions are a little silly, I suppose, but they still require asking. Admitting that the old, simplistic categories by which we've always tried to categorize fishermen are also silly should challenge us to rethink fishing as a very involved, deeply integrated activity in which any number of interests and urges are churning along together, pulling us one way or another and being generally ignored by our conscious minds. The next cast might have a different purpose than the previous one, say, if we hook a fish and decide all at once it would make a great dinner, or a great photograph, or just a great memory to share.

So when I think of Cornelius Hedges standing in the miserably cold shallows of Yellowstone Lake, harvesting fish for food, having some of the most memorable sport fishing of his whole life, and accumulating a publishable impression of the life and character of a soon-to-be-famous trout species, maybe I won't think of him as doing three things at once. Maybe I'll just think of him as a typically complicated sportsman, making the most of the circumstances.

Fly fishing, I would guess, is just another one of those

interesting multi-tasking endeavors in our lives, happily and uniquely developed in each of us. Best of all, when we fish, this whole array of complicated causes and effects can be running without interfering with the moment-to-moment joy of fishing. In fact, if we're doing it right, all those motives and rewards just hum right along in the background and make the joy even finer.

*By the time of Edward Hewitt's visit to Yellowstone, fishing was a
popular pastime in the park. F. Jay Haynes photographed these
fishers at West Thumb landing in 1896.*

Haynes Foundation Collection, Montana Historical Society
Photograph Archives, Helena

CHAPTER FOUR

Yellowstone II
Edward in Wonderland

Authorities darken counsel.

—George Edward McKenzie Skues,
The Way of a Trout with a Fly (1921)

"What boy of fifteen ever had his dream of adventure and sport better fulfilled than I when my father asked me to accompany him on a trip out West in a private car to visit Yellowstone Park? At that time this was a complete wilderness which had not yet been opened to the public."[1] Thus the famous fishing writer Edward Ringwood Hewitt, author of acknowledged mid-twentieth-century classics on trout and salmon fishing, began a childhood remembrance of his first Yellowstone fishing trip in the 1880s.

Hewitt, described by *Newsweek* shortly before his death in 1957 as "the last of the gentlemen scientist-naturalist-tinkerers," lived about as advantaged a life as an American could—perfect for a man of his remarkable energy and range of interests. Wealthy from birth (his grandfather was Peter Cooper, creator of the famous "Tom Thumb" locomotive), Hewitt held dozens of patents (he is credited with "inventing" the Mack Truck) and contributed significantly to fly-fishing theory and practice, including several important fly patterns.

Authority is a complicated business. The more candid profiles that his fellow anglers have written about him, while laudatory and even adulatory, reveal that Hewitt's most ardent admirers couldn't have been more impressed with him than he was with himself. Antiquarian angling book dealer John Moldenhauer recently wrote, "I think I would like to have fished with Hewitt; just once, and then briefly."[2] Hewitt's pronouncement shortly before he died that "I know more about trout than anyone else in the country" echoed the tone of much of his earlier writing.[3]

More than thirty years ago, when I began reading about fly fishing, I learned that Edward Ringwood Hewitt really was that kind of expert. In the writings of other fly-fishing experts, his was one of the most frequently invoked names— one of those people you just had to read. He was by all accounts one of the most important and influential of fly-fishing writers during the first half of the twentieth century. Among his many books, I heard most often about *Telling on the Trout* (1926), *Hewitt's Handbook of Fly Fishing* (1933), *Nymph Fly Fishing* (1934), *Secrets of the Salmon* (1922), and *A Trout and Salmon Fisherman for Seventy-Five Years* (1948).

This last title seemed, according to the authorities in the 1970s, to be his finest work, gathering the wisdom of *Telling on Trout* and *Secrets of the Salmon* into one generous volume. I had to have it right away, and, luckily, there was a handy 1972 reprint edition, which I still have today.

At the time, I was learning about fly fishing mostly just by doing it in Yellowstone Park, where I worked intermittently and played constantly. Imagine my surprise, then, when I opened Hewitt's masterwork and discovered that he, too, had fished the park. Imagine my greater surprise when I discovered that he didn't seem to have some of his facts quite straight. Such was the nature of fly-fishing authority, and my personal sense of abject ignorance, that I mentally glossed over these errors for a long time, not quite willing to admit that a card-carrying "Great" among angling writers could have gotten the simple details of this famous landscape so tangled up.

But over the years I often thought of Hewitt's Yellowstone stories. My own work as an ecological historian has led me deep into the early literature of the park, and in many ways Hewitt's reminiscence is much like those of countless other early visitors to this magical place. After a couple decades of research in this grayest of gray literature, I developed a forgiving feeling about the frequent shortcomings of the memoirs of these lucky souls who pioneered tourist travel in Yellowstone. After all, they were on vacation, or they were busy with their own adventures, or they were just not qualified to do any better. As a historian, I may have been disappointed by their unreliability, but who was I to judge them?

In that mood, I recently went back to Hewitt's account of Yellowstone. Though I still thought it enjoyable enough reading, I also found that his story was even more wrong than I remembered. His account of the boyhood trip, as well as of a second visit in 1914, is a fascinating historical study, not only for his enviable tales of catching truly extraordinary numbers of wild trout, but also for what we might politely call his lapses of memory.

In fact, in terms of historical accuracy, the whole thing is a mess. It's almost as if Hewitt unconsciously absorbed the tall-tale impulses of the mountain men who roamed this fantastic wilderness a few generations before he arrived. To Hewitt, reminiscing several decades after his trip, it all must have seemed even more amazing than it was.

Thanks to his famous self-confidence and to the romantic power of the West, Hewitt's memory magnified his own importance until his experiences and achievements were both heroic and unique. In reality, in the modern view, his achievements, especially his tremendous destruction of fish, were a little embarrassing. It is especially regrettable, as well, that his achievements were *not* unique; his behavior in those trout-rich days was all too common.

But let's start with young Edward on his first trip and learn more. He was, without question, correct that it was a great adventure. Today, not only boys of fifteen, but people of all ages would be thrilled to go where he went and have the fishing he had, to say nothing of getting to see and do all the other things he described.

GETTING TO THE FISHING, 1882

Yellowstone Park was created by act of Congress and signed into existence by President Ulysses S. Grant on March 1, 1872.[4] In the first decades of its existence, it was commonly known as "Wonderland" for all the marvels of geology and scenery that were found there. When Hewitt made his trip, the park had been "opened to the public" every summer since 1872 and had been receiving a small but steady flow of visitors—probably not more than a few hundred a year at first, but about one thousand a year by the time Hewitt arrived a decade or so later.[5] There can be no doubt that by the time he arrived for his visit, the park was already open for the summer season.

Hewitt's confusion in thinking the park was not opened apparently came from his traveling companions:

> My father had invited his old friend Sir John Pender, who was the leading owner of the Eastern Cable Co., to see something of our great United States. Included in the party were Senator Bayard, who was at the time Secretary of the Interior, Gen. Lloyd Bryce, and Captain Gorringe. . . . Senator Bayard thought that he ought to see the Park before he opened it to the public.[6]

Here we catch the flavor of young Edward's comfortable and well-connected life; this was indeed a distinguished party of important citizens. And here also, the errors continue. According to the redoubtable *Dictionary of American Biography*, Delaware U.S. senator Thomas Francis Bayard held his office from 1869 to 1885. He was never secretary of the Interior, though he was later secretary of state—a much more politically significant position—and ambassador to Great Britain. Hewitt was right to regard him as an important man.

Precisely what role Bayard might have had in the "opening" or management of Yellowstone Park is unclear. Contrary to Hewitt's apparent convictions that Bayard was somehow significant in Yellowstone's fortunes, the substantial published historical scholarship on the park is silent on Bayard. Though the park's various controversies and struggles over the past 130 years have been repeatedly studied in great detail—studies I have spent many years involved in myself— I find no mention of Bayard as even a minor player in those events.[7] But Hewitt's view of Bayard interests me, and I intend to poke around in the records a little more and see if I can learn more about any possible connections he may have had with Yellowstone.

In his published account, Hewitt didn't give a year for the trip, but he was born in New York on June 20, 1866, so for him to be fifteen, this trip probably occurred in 1881 or 1882.[8] A quick check of the annual report of the superintendent of the park for the year 1882 settled the question, and provided this tidbit about the party's makeup:

> United States Senator Bayard, of Delaware;
> Commander Gorringe, of the United States Navy;
> Lloyd S. Bryce, of New York City; Mr. Fuller, of
> London, England; and Mr. Merrill, of Philadelphia,
> with a cavalry escort, composed the Senator's party.[9]

Hewitt himself, being still a boy, apparently didn't merit mention in such distinguished company.[10]

Today's fly-fishing enthusiast can leave his apartment in

New York City first thing in the morning and be standing in one of my favorite fishing spots in Yellowstone by late afternoon. Before the coming of the railroads, the same trip took months, and even in Hewitt's time, when rails had not reached the park, the trip was time consuming and hard enough work to discourage many people. It took time to visit Yellowstone Park, and if you were from the East, it took money. Except for local visitors, the park's tourists tended to be upper-class people (the real "democratization" of the park experience began in 1915, when automobiles were allowed to enter the park).

According to Hewitt, the tracks had only reached a point in eastern Montana, somewhere near Billings, "a small frontier post. There we found Gen. Phil Sheridan encamped with his troops, who were returning from one of the minor Indian wars which he had just settled."[11]

One of the things that makes the study of Yellowstone history so delightful is that so many local events are well documented. On a surprising number of occasions, it is possible to cross-check someone's story (as by consulting the park superintendent's report to find out when Hewitt visited). It was easy to establish that Lieutenant General Philip Sheridan was indeed in the West that summer. He wasn't settling Indian wars, however. He was on an "exploration" jaunt that took him through much of the greater Yellowstone area, and he left us a nice official day-by-day report on it.[12]

Unlike Bayard, Sheridan is known to have been a concerned and influential participant in the early battles over the protection of Yellowstone Park. Inspecting conditions in the park was part of his mission that summer. He and his size-able party entered the greater Yellowstone area from the south, working their way up through Jackson Hole past the Teton Range, then through the park, which they left by way of what is now known as the Northeast Entrance. They then bushwhacked through some rugged country, down the Clarks Fork of the Yellowstone River, arriving at what he called "Billings Station," on the Yellowstone River, on August 31. They were now at or near the head of the rail line, and in a position to meet Hewitt's party, which, I assume, must have shown up at about the same time, in early September. (Hewitt does not say when during the summer his group visited.)[13]

Hewitt said that Billings, Montana, was "about three hundred miles from Yellowstone Park."[14] It was about 180. His party would travel up the Yellowstone Valley from Billings to the park's main (north) entrance by wagon, so it probably felt like 300. According to Hewitt, Sheridan "insisted that it would be unsafe to make the trip without an escort, as there might be roving bands of Indians which had not yet been returned to their reservations. He provided us with an escort of thirty cavalryman, together with two army supply wagons with four mules for each, and a buckboard with two horses for Senator Bayard."[15] By 1881 and 1882, the danger of Indian attack was relatively slight in the Yellowstone Valley, but the Battle of the Little Bighorn had occurred only six years earlier, and times were indeed nervous. Besides, the thought of Indian attack, even if mentioned only casually by Sheridan or his soldiers, probably would have had wild attraction to the boy Hewitt.

If Sheridan did provide the escort as protection from Indians, he certainly also provided it as an expected courtesy to prominent government officials and their guests. In any case, it seems most likely that these matters were all arranged well in advance, rather than being a spur-of-the-moment decision by Sheridan.[16]

Young Hewitt was having a ball. As the party proceeded up the Yellowstone Valley, they "camped near the Yellowstone River, where I had a fine chance to fish for trout. In those days the river teemed with fish, some of which I caught on a fly, but I soon found that grasshoppers made a much more effective lure. I had to fish fast to get enough trout for the camp of forty men. These trout seemed to run in size from two to four and a half pounds."[17]

Hewitt rightly identified the fish as cutthroat trout, as no local stocking of non-native trout had yet occurred. He fished for trout in stretches of the Yellowstone River where, thanks to a variety of human-caused changes, they are now comparatively scarce. It is unlikely, however, that a well-provisioned military escort for a party of prominent citizens and government officials was in any risk of running out of supplies if their fifteen-year-old dude angler happened to get skunked. I assume they were happy to incorporate Hewitt's catch into their camp fare, though. These were seasoned professional travelers, already well acquainted with the landscape and ready for all contingencies.

Hewitt's observations on the efficacy of grasshoppers was a common view of early anglers in this region, many of whom readily abandoned their artificial flies when the trout were in the least sullen and switched to grasshoppers. The Washburn Party, whose experiences are described in the previous chapter, would have agreed.

The abundance of grasshoppers helps date the trip. As I write this, in the first week of September in Yellowstone, the grasshoppers are thick and active along my local trout stream.

REACHING AND FISHING THE PARK

It would have taken the party several days to cover the 180 miles to the park. Hewitt wrote that the party "finally entered the Park at Mammoth Hot Springs, which at that time were a wonderful sight. When I visited them in 1914 they were sadly different and much smaller in extent and not so highly colored."[18]

Actually, they entered the park through the North Entrance, at the town of Gardiner, Montana, and then traveled five miles to Mammoth Hot Springs.

And actually, the hot springs had not diminished. Hewitt's boyhood memories, after thirty-odd years of gradual unconscious enhancement, simply enlarged the wonders he saw. This happens all the time. When I was working as a seasonal ranger-naturalist at Mammoth between 1972 and 1977, it was for me the number one question that repeat visitors had about the Mammoth area. They typically remembered the hot springs as bigger. In fact, the many, many outlets of the hot springs at Mammoth do change dramatically. Some dry up and others become active, and throughout the area, the surface features move around and rearrange themselves. This would have been reason enough for Hewitt not to recognize what he thought he remembered. But the total flow of the springs, and the total area covered by hot water (and thus by the colorful algae and bacteria that live in the water), would not have changed significantly. Like many others since, Hewitt probably remembered one or two outstanding thermal features that, upon his return, might even have dried up entirely; the water was simply emerging elsewhere.[19]

Once in the park, Hewitt continued his successful sport:

> Of course, we found the streams and lakes in the Park full of trout and I had no difficulty in keeping the camp supplied. There can be little doubt that on this trip I did the first fly fishing ever done in Yellowstone Park, and probably in the river.[20]

As my previous chapter shows, the earliest record of fly fishing in the present park area that I have seen dates from 1870.[21] Fly fishing was, in other words, going on in Yellowstone even before it was a park. Bozeman, Montana, the first sizeable community to develop near the park, had an active community of sportsmen, as well as commercial outlets for sporting goods, by the early 1870s, and the local newspaper reported regular outings from Bozeman over to the Yellowstone Valley to catch the famous and abundant trout. Why Hewitt would think that he was fishing in a social vacuum, and that there were no other sportsmen in Montana and Wyoming territories, is hard to guess, but I assume it's just more of the magnification of memory. Imagined Indian scares and the idea that the park was a wilderness not yet opened to the public were great tools of that magnification.

None of this is meant to take away from the incredible time that Hewitt must have had visiting Yellowstone back then. Hewitt's party apparently had their share of genuine outdoor adventures in the park. Hewitt said that a "grizzly bear nearly got me" and that he did shoot a mountain sheep for camp food, but failed to get an elk.[22] For reasons having nothing to do with fishing history and everything to do with the analysis of Yellowstone's wildlife history, I would love to find more details on those episodes.

Hewitt doesn't give us enough information to follow his route through the park, but most visitors had a few primary goals. They all sought to see the Grand Canyon of the Yellowstone and the larger geyser basins, and many wanted to spend some time at Yellowstone Lake. Hewitt's account is so brief that we just can't know where all he went, but from Mammoth Hot Springs he must have at least made his way down to the Midway Geyser Basin (then also known as Hell's Half Acre), for there he had a historically lucky break of the highest kind available to Yellowstone visitors. He got to see perhaps the most spectacular geyser anywhere in the world, then or now:

> Captain Gorringe and I saw the Imperial Geyser go off and narrowly escaped being hit by falling rocks. The explosion seemed to go about three hundred feet in the air and the water column looked as if it were one hundred and fifty feet in diameter.

This was a most awesome sight. This geyser was much larger than anything else in the Park and it only erupted for a few years and is now extinct. We saw it by accident, early in the morning.[23]

The only geyser named "Imperial" was not named until the 1920s. Instead, this was almost certainly a description of Excelsior Geyser, an astonishingly powerful feature that was active in the 1880s. Thanks to the many other visitors of that era who left accounts of the geysers, we know that Excelsior did indeed have such violent, huge eruptions.[24]

Hewitt and at least one other member of his party witnessed an eruption of Excelsior Geyser, the largest geyser in Yellowstone history. This eruption of Excelsior (above) happened in 1888.

F. Jay Haynes, photographer, Haynes Foundation Collection, Montana Historical Society Photograph Archives, Helena

This was an enormously enviable experience. Many modern Yellowstone enthusiasts would much rather see Excelsior in its glory days than have the fishing Hewitt had on that trip. Excelsior's eruption was by all accounts a thrilling, and even terrifying experience, and Hewitt was not exaggerating when he said they had to dodge rocks. This was a mighty hydrothermal force at work, which is possibly one reason why it didn't last very long; it may have blown out its own "plumbing" system with its powerful eruptions.

Hewitt does give us an intriguing clue about his possible route through the park, though it's not an especially certain one. His party encountered one of the groups of hide hunters that for about a decade had been decimating the herds of large mammals in the upper Yellowstone Valley. The hide hunters tended to do most of their work in the park's northern section, so this group of men could well have been anywhere across the park's "northern range," including the Lamar River Valley (which was off the main tourist route but may have appealed to the Bayard party for fishing and hunting opportunities). But they could have encountered the hide hunters in several other locations as well.

It's an interesting bit of information that Hewitt gives us here, in any case. Hide hunting, though against the rules (commercial killing of animals by professional hide hunters was distinguished from sport and subsistence killing of a few animals by park visitors, the latter being acceptable in part because there were so few hotels and other services), had probably peaked in the 1870s and was declining by 1882 as public sentiment, changing markets, and other factors affected the activities of these commercial game harvesters. But Hewitt saw the hide hunters at their successful worst:

> They had a wagon piled six feet high with skins—
> I do not know how many. Senator Bayard put a
> stop to this as soon as he returned to Washington.
> This was the last hunting in the Park.[25]

Here, Hewitt has again veered very near but not quite into the truth. The self-important tone ("my pal the Senator took care of this") is unfortunate, considering the true story of the ban on hunting in Yellowstone. This was a complicated effort, involving many people over a ten-year period. Hide-hunting was a scandal in Yellowstone by the mid-1870s— the subject of regional outrage, of editorials in the sporting press, and of great interest in the young conservation movement. Hunting, both for sport and hides, was banned in Yellowstone in 1883, not because of Senator Bayard, but because of all these forces, which were led by prominent eastern sportsmen, including George Bird Grinnell, then editor of *Forest and Stream*.[26] Hewitt's self-centered version of the story is correct only in the seriousness of the problem and the timing of the solution.

MORE DEAD FISH WEST OF THE PARK

Hewitt's party left the park "on the western side," presumably down the Madison Valley, crossing the park boundary north of the present site of the town of West Yellowstone, Montana.[27] He said they went that way "to make our way to the railroad."[28] This meant that they were headed over Targhee Pass into Idaho. West of the park, Hewitt continued to provide the party with trout and on occasion caught huge numbers of additional fish (as much as four or five hundred pounds of cleaned fish a day) for other people the party encountered. He may have reached his peak as a trout killer a few days later along the Snake River, during two days when he estimated he caught "from twelve hundred to fifteen hundred pounds of trout" in two days, for a band of Indians the party encountered.[29]

These are shocking numbers to the modern ear (and even if we admit that Hewitt might have been exaggerating them as he exaggerated other things, it's clear he killed huge numbers of fish). Hewitt, free to concentrate solely on killing fish, far outstripped the takes of the anglers in the Washburn Party of 1870. After reading even a few lines of his adolescent bragging about horse-loads of dead trout, we want to yell, "Ed! Ed! Get a grip! Put some back!" But Hewitt's experiences have a context we have lost in today's overpopulated world. When Hewitt made this trip, the conservation movement was young, the concept of the "fish hog" was still pretty new, and the West and its resources seemed endless to many people. Though generations of sportsmen had condemned the wholesale slaughter of game in the East, things felt different to many travelers in the western wilderness.[30]

There were practical concerns, too. Things hadn't changed all that much since the Washburn Party had to have fish to survive. Parties visiting Yellowstone were still in good part on their own. There were very few concessioners providing

*Large kills of fish were typical of fishing parties in
Yellowstone's first decades. The famous travel writer and lecturer
John L. Stoddard (in cap) and his party took this string of
cutthroat trout from Yellowstone Lake in 1896.*

F. Jay Haynes, photographer, Haynes Foundation Collection,
Montana Historical Society Photograph Archives, Helena

services of any kind, and the few that existed were often of
poor quality (the first large resort hotel wouldn't be built in
the park until 1883, at Mammoth, and even its construction
crews were fed the meat of wild animals). Visitors either had
to acquire their supplies catch-as-catch-can or provide for
themselves by hauling lots of food along or by hunting.
Hunting for camp food was legal in the park until 1883 for
that very reason. Hewitt's tremendous kills of fish may shock
us today, but they were just how things were done at the time.

Of course even in 1882, there were plenty of people who didn't like how things were done and who could see that the fish and wildlife resources were all too finite, but we had better admit that Hewitt had a great deal of justification for his behavior. After all, he was just a kid, no doubt encouraged in his behavior by his companions, who were prominent citizens with official government sanction. He was breaking no laws. That it was enormous fun only made it better.

And even Hewitt wasn't completely oblivious of the effects he was having. In his account of this trip, he concluded by pointing out that as soon as "a serious amount of fishing took place, the average size of the trout rapidly decreased in most of these western streams."[31] Right. So did the number of fish, though he did not mention that effect.

BACK AGAIN FOR BROWNS AND RAINBOWS, 1914

It is a little less easy to forgive Hewitt's similar behavior when he again visited the park, in 1914. By this time, the conservation movement had advanced significantly, and the excessive takes of thoughtless sportsmen were a matter of considerable attention and disapproval in sporting circles. But even though Hewitt again killed many fish in the park, it is apparently true that he was again operating legally. Still, the ethical realities were such that he might have known better when he undertook a fishing contest with one of the park's commercial fishermen:

> One day while we were stopping at the Old Faithful
> Inn I fished up the stream through the geyser basin,

trying, as so many do, to catch a trout in the brook and then turn and cook the fish in a hot spring before taking it off the hook. When I got above the geysers, there were plenty of good brown trout, and I caught a dozen or so which I laid out in front of the hotel when I came back. A man came up and asked me where I got them and told him, above the hotel on a dry fly. He seemed incredulous and wanted to see it done. It seems he was the professional fisherman who supplied the hotel with trout for the guests. He said he was going fishing the next morning and asked me to go with him to find out whether the dry fly or the wet fly was the better lure. In other words, he challenged me to a match—the only fishing match for numbers I ever took part in.[32]

Hewitt said that they "left early and went about six miles down the Madison River," which would have put them about twenty-one river miles from Old Faithful.[33] They fished hard until three in the afternoon, when they quit and counted fish:

When we returned to the Inn we laid out both catches on the ground and I found I had been beaten. He had 165 and I had 162, but the curious thing was that my fish taken on a dry fly averaged slightly larger than his. If the wind had not come I would certainly have gotten the most fish, as the dry fly is a better method of fishing such water than the wet fly. The professional was amazed that I could hold

Hewitt's route may have taken him past Gibbon Falls on the Gibbon River, a tributary of the Madison River famous for fly fishing.

From John Hyde, *Official Guide to Yellowstone National Park* (St. Paul: Northern News, 1887), p. 47

my own with him and said that I was the only easterner he had ever met who really knew how to fish.
I would just like to try that man again on a still day.[34]

Commercial fishing, even for hotel dinners, became illegal
in the park in 1917, though for many years after that the
hotel company still provided the pleasant courtesy of preparing the angler's own catch for dinner at a park restaurant.[35]

With that, Hewitt concluded his reminiscences of his old
Yellowstone fishing days. He leaves us both envious and a
little chagrined.

We envy the opportunities of such trips in such simple,
uncrowded times. Even in 1914, Yellowstone only received
about twenty thousand visitors—fewer than it sees now on
a single day in July.[36] Whether as anglers we prefer to fanta-
size about fishing unsuppressed native fish populations, or
fishing the explosively successful non-native fisheries created
in Yellowstone starting in the 1890s, we could imagine no
more perfect fishing trips than Hewitt took.

On the other hand, that young Hewitt could kill fish so
excessively in the 1880s, and again in 1914, is much more a
statement about his times than it is about him. That the leaders of his party 120 years ago could still be so insensitive to
the finite nature of fisheries populations is terribly revealing.
Notions of good behavior, ethical treatment of nature, and
moderate use of wild trout populations were all evolving
then, as they still are today. We should be grateful to Edward
Hewitt for the reminder that in each generation even the
most enlightened sportsmen and managers still have a lot to

A Day's Sporting, *from Herman Haupt's* Yellowstone National
Park *(New York: J. M. Stoddart, 1883, p. 51) suggests the sort
of mixed bag sportsmen might expect in Yellowstone at the time
of Hewitt's 1882 visit.*

learn, and still haven't achieved the understanding of natural
resources that their descendants will require.

We should also be grateful for the cautionary tale of over-
confidence we find in Hewitt's story. I'm not the first writer
to ponder the peculiar notion of authority in fishing writing.
The "fishing expert" has been the subject of skepticism and
ridicule for a long time (such as fishing writer Lefty Kreh's
famous observation that an expert is a guy more than fifty

miles from home with his own slide projector). After several centuries of intense theorizing by thousands upon thousands of bright, thoughtful people, fly fishers seem more divided than ever on many of the sport's theoretical and practical points. The publishing revolution that started in the 1970s and has continued ever since is viewed by many with great skepticism for its capacity to create instant if dubious authorities. At least one lesson of this mass of conflicting advice seems clear. There is, quite plainly, no single set of right answers, or right flies, or right attitudes, in sight—here is a laxness in the sport's personality that invites almost anyone to quite literally assume authority.

In fact, many of us are pretty sure that the irresolvability of its basic issues is part of what makes fishing so engaging. The point of several well-known fishing stories, including my novella *Shupton's Fancy* (1996), in which a man actually discovers a fly that will catch a fish on every cast, would seem to be that the last thing we need is perfection.

On the other hand, even recognizing the essential whimsy of the enterprise, we do like to think that our fly-fishing father figures measure up to certain minimum standards of reliability. Reading Hewitt on Yellowstone is like the first time while reading a magazine you've always been fond of, you come upon an article on a subject you know well and discover that the writer has the story all wrong. After the initial surprise, you wonder what else this magazine has been wrong about.

It is the peculiar nature of angling that, though we don't really expect our experts to solve all the problems, we do count on them to be better at it than we are, better enough that we can believe that on those occasions when we can't catch a certain fish, there are surely people around who can. Edward Ringwood Hewitt served that sort of role for generations of anglers.

WHATEVER BECAME OF EDWARD HEWITT?

Compiling and analyzing this early Yellowstone account has made me realize how much Hewitt's standing in the world of fly fishing has changed since I started fishing. When *A Trout and Salmon Fisherman for Seventy-Five Years* was reprinted in 1972, there was still a serious shortage of written advice on what we now consider basic topics, such as nymph fishing, or trout feeding behavior, or dry-fly techniques.

Now, by contrast, there are tons of books and a startling array of magazines, both national and regional. Most major fly-fishing areas and many individual rivers have entire books (to say nothing of websites) of their own. Hewitt, who in the mid-1970s was still being offered to us as the specialist's specialist, would now be regarded as a generalist. His books lack the local hatch charts, the dozens of carefully engineered local fly patterns, the rock-by-rock and pool-by-pool maps, and all the other rarified specifics that so many modern fly fishers thrive on. Hewitt's level of expertise has been more or less superceded, or at least marginalized, by the steady piling up of more and more information about more and more places.

Like his longtime rival author, George LaBranche, and like the great trout-fishing generalist Ray Bergman, Edward

Ringwood Hewitt still has his admirers among the older angling readers, but for the most part, his lessons and tales have been left behind, or built on so deeply that most people don't even recognize that there is a foundation under what they are learning. Hewitt's fade into obscurity shows the extent to which a sense of history, even history so recent it is more the "current events" of our own life span, is not seen as an important commodity in the modern marketing of fly fishing.

Historian Ken Owens has done important work in placing similar western angling experts, now largely neglected, in context. His account of Idahoan Ted Trueblood, longtime *Field and Stream* regular in the 1950s, 1960s, and 1970s, shows a western parallel for the eclipse of Hewitt. Trueblood, a workhorse outdoor writer with a wonderful common touch, not only instructed his readers well in the basics, he taught them conservation values, alerted them to new technology, and became a popular role model for generations of new eastern and western anglers. Owens says that "no person did more to bring on the 1970s fly-fishing boom in the northern Rockies" than Trueblood.[37] Besides all that, Trueblood was, in contrast to Hewitt, a really nice guy, one of those old-shoe-familiar characters who just naturally generated a large, affectionate following. Like Hewitt, he taught a lot of people how to fish and showed them why it was such a good life.

The question that naturally arises at this point is, of course, who cares? If we've left their theoretical approach behind or improved on it so much that we don't need to read them anyway, what's the point of exhuming these musty old geezers and reading stuff we're already beyond?

And the answers to those questions are the same ones as always. We probably haven't left them behind at all; we just don't know how much they matter.

And, on a more fundamental level, if you can only measure the worth of reading a book by its most superficial gimmee-value—by its capacity to satisfy some short-term need or greed—then you probably don't understand reading, much less fly fishing, anyway, and I can't help you.

Since the establishment of Yellowstone National Park in 1872, Minerva Terrace, part of the Mammoth Hot Springs complex of thermal features, has on several occasions become completely inactive and then reactivated. Changing conditions among the features at Mammoth no doubt explain Hewitt's erroneous statement that by the time of his 1914 visit to Yellowstone, the springs at Mammoth were greatly diminished from their appearance in 1882.

Yellowstone National Park, National Park Service

But the doubters might then counter with this harder question: Haven't you just proved that Hewitt was a blowhard and not very reliable? What kind of guy is that for us to spend time reading?

I admit that there's something to that. Hewitt, I have shown, often got it wrong. In his Yellowstone stories, he sounded way too proud of himself. But he still had something, and it's something we can never match or capture without him. Like Trueblood and quite a few others who are neglected now among both western and eastern readers, Edward Ringwood Hewitt was *there*. I never read him without remembering that, and being grateful that for all his self-centered blather he managed to leave me so many of his own memories of what it was like, and why it all mattered.

Pteronarcys californica, *the giant stone fly popularly known*
as the salmonfly, is western fly fishing's most famous aquatic
insect. It was originally identified for science from a California
specimen, but it is now best known for its abundance on many
Rocky Mountain streams.

Courtesy Glenda Bradshaw

CHAPTER FIVE

Dark Stones and Devil Scratchers

*I had nothing else to do, so I caught salmon flies in my
landing net. I made up my own game. It went like this:
I couldn't chase after them. I had to let them fly to me.
It was something to do with my mind. I caught six.*

—Richard Brautigan, *Trout Fishing in America* (1967)

I first saw salmonflies just a few years after Richard
Brautigan told a couple million Americans about them in his
quirky little book. I was walking up Callendar Street in
Livingston, Montana, a good half a mile from the Yellowstone
River, when I became aware of them. Perhaps they'd been
there before and I hadn't been paying attention, or perhaps
they'd just arrived that minute; Livingston is almost as
famous for its winds as it is for its fishing. But the flies were
everywhere. Some were rattling by above the traffic, some
were being squashed beneath it. They were huge, the kind of
thing you'd reflexively bat away if you didn't know what
they were. Even if you did, you might.

I was new to fly fishing. To that point, my fly selection was
limited to the dozen or so general patterns that my brother in
Michigan gave me, along with a rod and reel, when he

learned I was about to move to the Rockies. The salmonfly was a whole new thing, and an imitation of it was such an obviously good idea that soon I was heaving store-bought Sofa Pillows (Pat Barnes's very popular imitation) and my own crude variations on the Sofa Pillow theme onto every stream I saw, regardless of water size, habitat types, or known fly life.

I discovered that in the small, uncelebrated freestone streams that I fished most, a big, long orangish-reddish dry fly was an all-season tool, good from the earliest days of the hatch well into fall. Whether the fish took them for salmonflies, grasshoppers, or something else, they worked. The various dry fly patterns of the salmonfly often sank and came swimming back to me like punk Muddlers, but that didn't matter much either. And of course the big nymph imitations—from the chenille Montana Nymph to Charlie Brooks's large-caliber, heavily weighted monsters—were good from opening day on.

My experience with salmonflies crudely mirrors their history in western fly fishing. It took a little while for the fly to assume an important place in the fly fisher's arsenal, but then it became central to the whole enterprise. Now that's changed again, and I'm not sure what's next.

Discovering the Animal

The insect in question, *Pteronarcys californica,* was originally described in the *Journal of the Linnean Society of London* in 1848 (in which it was "*Pteronarcys californicus*"). I assume that any fishermen who found them before that didn't need a scientific designation to recognize them as great trout food.

(I am still looking for Native American history or lore related to them.)

The original description is in an odd Latin-like text, but after only forty years I seem to have forgotten everything from my three years of high school training in that lovely language. And even a casual glance suggests that this wasn't written in anything like the Latin that Miss Hedges tried so valiantly to teach me. Here's the original, beginning with a revision of "generic characters of *Pteronarcys*":

PTERONARCYS, Newm.

CHAR. GEN. *Segmenta thoracica* etiam in Imagine branchiis externis prædita. *Alæ* magnæ, reticulatæ. *Palpi maxillares* labialibus multò longiores, 5-articulati; articulis 2 basilibus brevibus, reliquis elongatis, externè dilatatis. *Mandibulæ* parvæ, obtusæ. *Segmentum abdominale* octavum in mari processu longo ventrali munitum, in fœminâ paulò evolutum vel bifidum. Mr. Newport added the following new species:—

PTERONARCYS CALIFORNICUS [♂]; capite thoraceque saturatè brunneis, fronte clypeo labroque rufis, oculis ocellisque nigris, segmentis thoracicis lineâ longitudinali interruptâ flavâ, abdomine aurantiaco lateribus brunneis, stylis caudalibus basi flavis, antennis pedibusque totis atris, alis obscuris nigro-nervosis sed absque maculâ stigmali.

Hab. in Californiâ (*D. Hartweg*).[1]

I asked a Canadian friend, medievalist Richard Hoffmann, of York University, to take a shot at translating the Latin in this little description. Richard, who has done so much to clarify the early history of fly fishing in Europe, and who, not surprisingly, is a skilled and enthusiastic fly fisher himself, obliged. He characterized the description as "composed in an odd Latin, almost halfway between Latin and English." Anyway, this is what he got (bracketed comments are Richard's):

GENERIC CHARACTERISTICS. Even in the adult the thoracic segments provided with external "branches" [i.e., gill filaments]. Wings large, reticulate ["netted"]. Maxillary palps by far longer than the labials, 5-jointed; with two basal joints short, spreading outwards. Mandibles small, blunt. Eighth abdominal segment in the male built up on the belly with a long projection, in the female spread out a little or forked ["split in two parts"]. . . .

PTERONARCYS CALIFORNICUS male; head and thorax deep with brownish, forepart of the "shield" and labrum reddish, eyes and ocelli black, thoracic segments with broken yellow longitudinal line, abdomine golden ["gilded"?] with the sides brownish, caudal points wih yellow base, antennae and feet [legs?] all dull black, wings shadowed with veiny black but without distinguishing marks.

Habitat in California (D. Hartweg).[2]

The people whose names were associated with the description of this insect that would become so momentous in western fishing were momentous themselves. Edward Newman (1801–1876), a British entomologist and botanist, author of books on birds' nests and eggs, ferns, moths, and butterflies, was founder of a magazine, *Zoologist*. He described the genus *Pteronarcys* in 1838. George Newport (1803–1854), a prominent entomologist "distinguished for his research in insect anatomy and comparative anatomy," completed a term as president of the Entomological Society shortly before this description appeared.[3] He apparently prepared the formal published description of *Pteronarcys californica*.

The "D. Hartweg" mentioned in parentheses at the end has been a little harder to pin down. The reason for trying is that it is my best guess that he is the person who actually collected the specimen upon which this description is based. The exasperating vagueness of the site location ("Habitat in California," for Pete's sake, as if that's enough detail!) has led me on an only partly successful search for more precision.

Thanks to Miss Gina Douglas, librarian and archivist at the Linnean Society of London, I was alerted to the career of one Theodore Hartweg (1812–1871), a widely published naturalist who was sent by the Horticultural Society of London on a botanizing expedition to Mexico and California at just the right time. Hartweg arrived in Mexico in November 1845 and spent all of 1846 and 1847 in arduous, slow travel across Mexico, up to California, and back to Mexico, before returning to London in early 1848.[4] This trip was made all the more adventurous and complicated by the war between Mexico and the United States, which he walked into the middle of and which occasionally stranded him or restricted his movements.

It's kind of nice to think of the salmonfly, this great symbol of western fly fishing, as having come to the attention of science in such turbulent days—a real "Wild West" debut, so to speak—but even without a war swirling around him, Hartweg's journey featured more than enough perils and hardships.

Hartweg, despite that vexing disagreement between his first name and the initial in the species description (is the "D." an initial, or does it stand for "described by," or "Doctor," or something else?), seems a most promising candidate as possible collector of the specimen, even though his extended published journal of the expedition speaks of hundreds of plant species collected without mentioning any other collections. It seems unlikely that such a determined naturalist would have passed up opportunities to collect at least some other specimens, especially such relatively easy-to-transport ones as insects. The man certainly spent a fair amount of time near rivers, and the coincidences of his visit to *Pteronarcys* country—in timing, location, and similarity of name—seem too great to ignore.[5] Further improving the odds that he is our man, in 1851, when George Newport described another American stone fly, *Pteronarcys regalis,* he mentioned that "the following new species has recently been brought by Mr. Hartweg from California," adding at the conclusion of the description the notation "Hab. In California, D. Hartweg."[6]

So until I learn more, I will assume that Theodore Hartweg collected the salmonfly. He was in California at just the right time, and his travels took him to a variety of drainages in the upper Sacramento Valley, where it seems almost certain he must have been in the appropriate habitat for *Pteronarcys californica*. He could well have shipped the specimen home along with some of his other collections, allowing it to arrive in plenty of time for the published analysis and description.

I only wish we knew which river the specimen came from, or even which specific reach of which river. As big a deal as the salmonfly later became to fishermen, it almost seems like there ought to be a little sign there or something.

MAKING FLY TYING WESTERN

Even though fly fishing was being practiced widely in the western United States in the mid- to late 1800s, at first most of the fishermen did what I did when I first got here—they relied on general patterns they ordered or brought from the East. I'm also sure that some anglers started tying their own variations pretty quickly, but if the published accounts of fly fishing in the West in the late 1800s are any indication, most fishermen still leaned toward the old standards—the Coachman, Professor, Montreal, Parmacheene Belle, Gray Hackle, and other popular patterns. I assume that in larger sizes some of these might sometimes have imitated the salmonfly well enough to satisfy the relatively undiscriminating native trout.

In his thoughtful overview of western fly-fishing history, *Cutthroat and Campfire Tales* (1988), John Monnett has suggested that westerners in the late 1800s may have favored certain dull-colored traditional patterns for practical reasons:

Continuous generic references to "Grey Hackle, Brown Hackle, and Coachmen" flies are abundant in newspaper and periodical reports of the era, indicating that patterns tended to be subdued. This trend may not have been the result of trying to imitate western insects exactly. More likely it was because brightly colored avian resources were simply scarce. Undoubtedly "fancy" Victorian wet fly patterns from the East found their way into the fly books of western anglers after about 1870, but there is surprisingly little mention of them before the last decade of the nineteenth century.[7]

There is something to this, but we have to be careful about imagining the West of 1880, or even of 1870, as being deprived of access to anything the East had. Once the transcontinental railroads were running, beginning in 1869, you could get anything you could pay for, and fly fishermen have usually been able to pay for things they want. Western fly fishing stopped being a pioneer adventure soon after there were stagecoaches and trains stopping regularly in the neighborhood.

As far as western preferences for fly patterns, my own impression from reading great amounts of this nineteenth-century material is that by the 1880s at least some western anglers, whether resident or tourist, actually concluded that muted colors worked best. That certainly was the opinion of at least one visitor, Rudyard Kipling, after fishing Wyoming and Colorado and talking with local fishermen in 1889:

If ever any man works the Western trout-streams, he would do well to bring out with him the dingiest flies he possesses. The natives laugh at the tiny English hooks, but they hold, and duns and drabs and sober greys seem to tickle the aesthetic tastes of the trout.[8]

Kipling seems to have encountered the salmonfly himself, judging from the near-raving excitement of his account of fishing Yankee Jim Canyon on the Yellowstone River (see page 18), where he found the "water-willow crowded with the breeding trout fly" in early July. Obviously, some people (the natives he mentioned) disagreed over fly pattern or hook size. But they knew what worked for them, too.

If you look through the popular American fly-pattern books of that era, say, for example, the grandest of them all, Mary Orvis Marbury's *Favorite Flies and Their Histories* (1892), you will be hard pressed to find many, if any, patterns that you could call close imitations of the salmonfly, either the adult or the nymph.[9] But you will find any number of reports from western anglers who were having great successes (even allowing for reportorial excess) with the "classic" form and colors of the Victorian wet fly.

Western fishermen were noticing things that probably had to do with the big stone flies, though. The Marbury book was composed in good part of letters from anglers all over the country to the Orvis Company, describing their favorite flies. One of Orvis's correspondents, W. P. Webster of Salt Lake City, did his fishing in Idaho, Yellowstone Park, and the Gunnison River in Colorado. He recommended the Professor

The West's first fly fishers started with fly patterns popular in the East. This fly plate from Mary Orvis Marbury's Favorite Flies and Their Histories *(1892) featured typical wet flies of the day. Fly number 192, second row from the top, far left, The Professor, was recognized as a likely imitation of the western salmonfly.*

and the Dark Stone but said that "in this locality, any fly, salmon-color in appearance, is good."[10] The Dark Stone, as Marbury illustrated it, has yellow rather than orange ribbing, but it's a big, slate-gray wet fly that I would willingly use during the salmonfly hatch. Webster's simple advice seems to suggest that he, like me so many years later, used "salmon-color" flies through much of the season.

J. V. Nye, of Nye City, Montana, sent Orvis a fly he called "the Yellowstone trout fly," saying it resembled "a fly that we have here in June and July." Marbury somewhat disappointedly footnoted this passage, saying that "the fly inclosed was a Professor, tied on a No. 7 hook."[11] We could hopefully overinterpret and second-guess our way into this historical moment, pointing out that the Professor's yellow body might have done justice to some of the smaller stone flies, or somehow even suggested something about the pale colors on the salmonfly itself—but that's all just recreational speculation.

It is safe to assume that the standard wet-fly patterns, indeed the whole stylized approach to fly patterns represented by those flies, were as good as anything else in the West for the same reason they worked so well in the East. Prior to the widespread planting of European brown trout, there was much less call for studious imitation of natural insects in trout streams. Western cutthroat trout, most of them anyway, were even easier to catch than eastern brook trout. Though there are accounts of cutthroat trout being uncatchable on artificial flies in those early days (such as the experiences of the Washburn Party and Edward Hewitt, recounted in earlier chapters), the preponderance of historical material makes it clear that such occasions were the exception. It wasn't until after the brown trout arrived, fishing pressure increased, and angling became more difficulty thereby, that the average American angler would begin to develop an approach to fly fishing that included a serious interest in imitating local insects. A few thoughtful eastern anglers had shown interest in hatch-matching before, but it wasn't a big deal until it became generally necessary.[12] New fish species and greatly increased fishing pressure both made it so. But, with its smaller human population and far lighter fishing pressure, all this took longer in the West.

Meanwhile, the salmonfly was undoubtedly getting better known. In 1881, Philetus Norris, superintendent of a very young Yellowstone Park, described fishing in the Grand Canyon of the Yellowstone, "a stream we found literally filled with delicious trout of rare size and beauty, and so gamy that all desired of them were caught at each of our visits of this year, during our brief nooning, using as bait some of the countless salmonflies which were crawling upon the rocks or on our clothing, upon hooks fastened to one end of a line, the other being merely held in the hand or attached to some chance fragment of driftwood; but the sport seemed harder upon the hooks and lines than upon the trout, which were abundant, both in the river and out of it, after the loss of all our lines."[13] Thank heavens later superintendents learned to write shorter sentences, but even today they might discover action like that in the canyon.

Norris's mention of the salmonfly is, by the way, the earliest use I have found of that term. I assume that Norris was not the

*Philetus Norris, Yellowstone's colorful second superintendent
(he was from Michigan, but loved to affect a mountain-man
image), used the term "salmon flies" as early as 1881,
but it is not known who originated this name for
the big western stone flies.*

Yellowstone National Park, National Park Service

first to describe the giant stone fly as a salmonfly because his matter-of-fact use of the term suggests it was already common.

A few years later, one of Yellowstone's most respected early outfitters, Elwood "Uncle Billy" Hofer, wrote about the state of the park's trout fishing in *Forest and Stream*:

> On about the 10th of July trout or salmon flies began to appear. These are the best bait to be found for taking fish; they are winged insects some two inches long when full grown. We have no angle worms in this country, but nature has kindly given us the salmon fly and the grasshopper. I have often noticed that when a "true sportsman" can't catch fish with artificial flies he will take very kindly to grasshoppers and salmon flies. One will often see a fisherman after a festive grasshopper, striking wildly at it with a hat profusely ornamented with artificial flies.[14]

Here again is the by-now almost knee-jerk ridicule of the fly fisher whose flies don't work as well, or even work at all, compared to natural baits. But substitute only artificial salmonflies and artificial grasshoppers in Billy's remarks, and it sums up my own angling philosophy during my first few years in the West. If I had salmonfly imitations, both nymph and adult, and grasshopper imitations, I figured I could do pretty well through most of the season.

Considering that the fly was first scientifically identified from a specimen collected in California, I have wondered if the name "salmonfly" might in some local way have been related to the arrival time of a run of salmon in a given river where the flies emerged at the same time. But most people used the term in reference to the distinctive salmon-flesh-colored markings on the body of the adult. As late as 1925, biologist Richard Muttkowski, in a study of "The Food of Trout in Yellowstone National Park," repeatedly referred to *Pteronarcys californica* as the "salmon-colored stone fly" and observed that they and their smaller stone fly kin were "the most conspicuous fish food item in the Yellowstone streams."[15]

But most western fishermen already knew that. They called them salmonflies, willow flies, trout flies, and who knows what all else, just as they called the nymph of the same insect helgrammites, devil scratchers, caddis, and other lively but scientifically indefensible names. Whatever they called them, they knew them well and were ready when imitation of them started to matter more.

CRAFT

The thing that most truly distinguishes fly fishing from all the other sports and games is the extent to which the individual fly fisher personally creates an important part of the necessary equipment. There are, of course, hunters who build their own bows, reload their own shells and cartridges, or even build their own rifles, just as there are no doubt baseball players who turn out their own bats on a lathe or snowshoers who craft their own snowshoes. But it seems certain that proportionately more fly fishers tie flies than practitioners of other sports similarly take on the construction of any equivalent item they need.

This is no small distinction. It adds greatly to the personal engagement of the individual if he has such a powerful stake in the enterprise. Tying your own fly is investing yourself. You catch a fish more completely, and personally, with a fly you tied.

As important, when you sit down to tie a fly, you take a seat at a very large, very old table. As you go through the magazines, books, and videos—taking or ignoring advice, learning tricks and shortcuts, discerning and taking sides in old debates, then picking and choosing a pattern, a style, eventually even an aesthetic stance—you participate in a long, complicated, and apparently endless conversation over those and many other matters. You join not merely a club, but a guild.

Fly tying is thus a distinct passion within the sport of fly fishing. It is a matter of continuing wonder to me that even after all these centuries of invention there seems to be no slackening in the subtle and even pronounced variations we can cook up, in fresh ways, to attach feathers, furs, and many other materials to a hook.

I'm convinced we sometimes look a little demented, sitting there at the fly-tying vise, but that's predictable as the outsider's view of any obscure and vaguely nerd-like activity. In fact, in our own little realm, we're off on a great, exciting, historically buttressed quest. We are both slaves to tradition and rebels against the establishment that tradition always tends to sustain, and out of that tension comes some authentically enticing combination of creativity, frustration, and reward. We can't resist.

It is a matter of almost equal wonder that our excitement

over this little craft seems never to slacken, generation to generation, though it was long ago established that for the practical purpose of catching fish you can do just fine with a few established patterns in a few standard sizes. But I shouldn't be so surprised, because fly tying, like fishing itself, is well known for its nurturing of that most seductive of emotions: hope. We can't resist.

It's rather like music. Listen to a pianist run chromatically through the three octaves in the middle of the keyboard, and you have heard all the notes—less than forty of them—that are available to most songwriters. If you were somehow brand new to music, you would never dream that after millennia of hard effort we could still be in no danger of exhausting the possibilities for new and interesting melodies.

I suppose that's the measure of any good craft, art, or other absorbing human pursuit—it pulls us in and hooks us as much for its possibilities as for its immediate rewards. At least it's clear that something of that sort happened to Montana's fly tiers in the early 1900s as they released themselves from dependence upon the commercial fly patterns and fly-tying traditions of the East.

WEAVERS OF LIFE

It has been called the golden age of trout fishing in Montana. Starting shortly after the turn of the century and continuing well into the 1930s, Montana anglers experienced a kind of fishing right out their front doors that today's top-end, world-traveled angler would spend a fortune, and travel far, to obtain. Even during the depression, which hit Montana harder than it hit many states, some great things were happening along the rivers. There were lots of fish, as browns and rainbows, recently introduced in several major drainages, established themselves and grew fat and strong. There were few people, as the state had not yet been discovered by hoards of tourists and anglers.

And there were some very inventive fishermen. New flies and new ideas were everywhere, as western anglers came into their own with patterns and techniques suited to the waters. No longer did they simply order flies from "back East."

In Missoula, starting about 1927, Norman Edward Means developed a new "bug" series for trout fishing. Means, known throughout the state by his nickname Paul Bunyan, marketed his "Bunyan Bugs" widely, providing Montana fishermen with a great imitation of the large western stone flies. In his fictional memoir *A River Runs Through It,* Norman Maclean has his narrator recall his first sight of a Bunyan Bug, fifty years before: "I took one look at it and felt perfect."[16]

The Bunyan Bug exemplifies the rampant unorthodoxy of this regional school of fly tying. The bugs were not "tied" at all. Their bodies were carved from wood, horsehair wings were stuck into the sides at right angles from the body, and the thing was painted any of a variety of colors, to coarsely imitate any of several splay-winged insects. In fact, all were just scaled-up or scaled-down versions of the same pattern, and it seems beyond question that the whole series was inspired by the need for some really big, durable, buoyant lure to imitate the salmonfly itself.

But there were those who preferred orthodoxy. After about

Norman Means originated his Bunyan Bug, an unorthodox wood-and-horsehair floating fly, in the 1920s. Though he tied it in a variety of sizes and colors, the salmonfly was probably the primary inspiration for the whole series.

Courtesy Doug O'looney

1932, Californian Don Martinez was coming up to West Yellowstone every summer to run a fly shop. He eventually popularized such famous patterns as the Woolly Worm, an ancient fly he brought to its modern form.[17]

Martinez is a fascinating and colorful character about whom we still know too little. Thanks to a wonderfully candid correspondence between him and eastern angler-entomologist Preston Jennings in the early 1940s, we get some lively glimpses of an early western fly-tying pioneer at work. As an undergraduate, Martinez had at least some exposure to limnology and entomology, and he was well read in the British fishing literature. Had he chosen another region for his fly shop, he no doubt would now be remembered as a serious imitationist; he much preferred small, reasonably precise fly patterns based on his own observations of natural insects. He made insect collections of his own on Yellowstone-area streams, even attempting watercolor portraits of them, but regarded the whole effort as a failure compared to more disciplined collections being made by other anglers elsewhere.[18]

The problem he faced was that the demand among his customers was almost entirely for big, rough, and fairly generalized patterns. He was often frustrated by the fly fishers who came into his shop. Some he found to be overdressed pretentious snobs caught up in the social status of being dry-fly fishermen. Others were just ignorant hicks or, as he described them to Jennings, "club-footed peasants."[19]

Martinez seemed not to fish the salmonfly hatch much himself, but by 1941 he offered a couple generalized imitations, the Red Squirrel Tail and the Bloody Butcher, both long-shanked over-sized dry flies that, as far as Martinez was concerned, were mostly effective because of the silhouette of their long squirrel-tail wings.[20] Both were quite similar in conformation and materials to Pat Barnes's famous Sofa Pillow, which Pat tied for the first time shortly after World War II (and which was a staple of my early salmonfly fishing thirty years later).[21] This makes me assume that the general Sofa Pillow idea had probably been drifting around that part of Montana for some time.

Over in Livingston, Dan Bailey, who started coming out

Pat Barnes, for many years a popular West Yellowstone,
Montana, guide and fly tier, was among the first to develop a
salmonfly imitation, the Sofa Pillow, in the style of a traditional,
if oversized, dry fly. He's shown here on the Missouri River
being rowed by Paul Roos.

Courtesy Doug O'looney

from New York in the 1930s, was on his way to becoming the
most famous western angler of them all and staying that way
well into the 1970s. He was rapidly developing new flies and
modifying traditional fly patterns to fit the new western conditions. Bailey, thoroughly grounded in eastern lore and traditions yet eminently practical, provided the clearest connection
with older ways. Though he kept in touch with his eastern
friends, including Preston Jennings, he largely abandoned
the detailed hatch-matching that was at that time occupying
the attention of Jennings, Art Flick, Charles Wetzel, Vincent
Marinaro, and many other eastern anglers at the approach
of mid-century. As Jennings's widow said, "Dan wasn't much
interested in this technical side of fly tying. He was an

*Dan Bailey (standing, center), who learned his fly-tying skills in
the East, came west in the 1930s. He adapted his skills to western
waters and turned his small Livingston, Montana, fly business into
one of the world's best-known tackle shops, where anglers could
not only shop for western flies, but could also watch them being
tied by professionals. Shops like Bailey's became great crossroads
of anglers, as well as of fly-tying theories.*

Bill Browning, photographer, Montana Historical Society
Photograph Archives, Helena

empiricist who loved the fishing—and big attractor flies."[22]

Empiricism was what the rivers of Montana demanded
then. And, though Bailey became world renowned as a western fisherman (ironically, much more famous than many
native westerners), he was only one of many pioneer fly fishers in Montana, men who saw the opportunities and the
challenges and who knew when to leave old ideas behind

and go in search of new ones. Out of that search grew one of the most unusual and innovative fly-tying traditions in the known history of the sport. It is the tradition of the fly weavers.

Though there is some question who first developed techniques for weaving animal hair into flies, there is no doubt who established the tradition that would last: Franz B. Pott, whose series of "Mite" flies are still sold in some Montana shops.

Pott was a barber and a wig-maker by trade. George Grant, the leading historian of Montana angling and himself the most famous craftsman in the fly-weaving tradition, believes that Pott's background in dealing with hair gave him a natural edge in creating woven-body flies: "Pott was originally a barber and a wig-maker, and he used his knowledge of the latter profession to conceive the woven-hair hackle, the one factor that sets his flies apart from all similar imitations, of which there have been more than a few. When he first tied his woven hair hackles some fifty years ago, I do not believe he was primarily interested in the superiority of hair over feather as a hackle material. It is my opinion that because he was formerly a wig-maker he merely applied his knowledge of hair weaving to the making of hackles and found it to be an excellent way to attach hair to a hook shank."[23]

Whether he was first or not, when he switched from human-hair wigs to badger-hair wet flies, Pott led the way for later fly weavers, being the first to patent his methods in a pair of patent applications approved in 1925 and 1934. Soon others were varying the weaves and patterns, and Montana trout were introduced to flies unlike those seen by trout anywhere else in the world.

In the 1920s, Franz B. Pott, the original Montana innovator in woven-hair flies, developed a series of Mite patterns that relied heavily on a stylized approach to the salmonfly.

Courtesy Doug O'looney

The woven-hair fly is a complex little item. The body is formed by any of a host of methods of cross-weaving strands of hair (badger, skunk, deer, and others) back and forth around the hook, often over a flat wire frame or foundation that has been lashed to the hook to conform to the flattened shape of many nymphs. The hackles are also woven, most often by weaving individual hairs or groups of hairs in a series along a thread line. Most of the early woven flies were fished wet, but years later Grant would perfect a hackle for dry flies, woven of deer hair.

The weaving-and-wrapping process brings to mind something more formal and daunting than fly tying—it crosses a line into architecture, or at least basketry. It has been this complexity of construction that has kept most fly tiers from trying to tie the flies. Some patterns take even the experts half an hour to complete, when a good commercial fly tier must be able to crank out twenty or more in an hour just to stay in business. Though Montana's most famous fly weavers were themselves professionals, and though some of them seemed to make a tolerable living at it, there was no denying that there were quicker, easier ways to make effective flies.

But fly fishing is too complex itself to reduce any one element of it to such simple terms. The weavers tied the flies because they worked, people liked them and were willing to pay for them, and they caught trout. Pott was kept busy even though he had to price his flies at three for a dollar. This was back when even at bloated New York prices you could get a dozen high-quality standard trout flies for that much money.

Many Montana anglers wanted woven flies, though, so the tiers kept at it. In Butte, Wilbur Beatty developed a small factory with a staff of women who mass-produced woven-hair flies. Dan Bailey created his own variation, the excellent "Mossback" series that imitate the nymphs of the smaller western stone flies. Bailey's patterns were perhaps more truly imitative than most of the other woven flies. The Mossback is, in shape and outline, obviously a stone fly nymph imitation. It had the added attraction of being available in two-tone versions, in keeping with the "countershading" so common among many wild animals and suggesting a much lighter belly that, I think, many nymphs don't actually have.[24]

But precision imitation wasn't really the point. Most of the patterns developed by Pott, Beatty, and the others were not realistic. Most of them had the hair hackle—presumably what the fish take to be legs—sprouting in a collar that encircled the hook just behind the fly's head. Stylistically, these early woven-haired flies placed the basic elements of a traditional fly in the same conformation or profile as had other wet-fly tiers for centuries. The early ones weren't even tied on the long-shanked hooks that are now regarded as essential to achieve the correct, extended proportions of the salmonfly.

But this was apparently no real disadvantage. Whether the tier or the angler knew it or not, a smaller version of such a fly, with its pronounced, splaying hackle of hair emerging from its shoulder, may just as easily have been imitating an emerging mayfly or, even more probably, a caddis fly.

The flies were also bulky, even stout, with none of the supple grace or indistinctness of silhouette that seems to characterize so many of the insects the trout were eating. Who could say if this was an advantage or a disadvantage?

The combination of qualities that the flies did have, though, was good enough for early- to mid-century Montana trout. There was ample durability and an undeniable bugginess that satisfied lots of trout. The Sax & Fryer store in Livingston, which, among many other services, sold anglers the Mite flies for much of the twentieth century, maintained records of large trout taken locally; most of the largest fly-caught fish, up to about ten pounds, were taken on the Pott flies.[25]

THE MASTER

But for all their pioneering and popularity, these early weavers were in a way just a prologue for what would later become of a craft at the hands of George Grant. He has become the most successful proponent, the most honored practitioner, and the most careful historian of the woven-hair fly. Grant took the fairly simple, even primitive techniques of his predecessors and over his seventy-year career as a tier made them increasingly sophisticated. More important, he made them famous.

I was fortunate enough to get to know George in the late 1970s, when he wrote a series of historical articles for *The American Fly Fisher*, the journal of the Museum of American Fly Fishing (now the American Museum of Fly Fishing), of which I was director. George was born in Butte in 1906, when the town was a wide-open mining center that historian

Montanan George Grant, pictured on his beloved Big Hole River in the 1930s and the 1980s, took full advantage of a spell of unemployment as a young man to launch a career as a fly tier and theorist that would by the 1970s bring him renown as the master of fly-weaving techniques.

Courtesy Todd Collins (left) and Mike Gurnett, photographer, Montana Fish, Wildlife and Parks, Helena (right)

Joseph Kinsey Howard called "the black heart of Montana
. . . a monument to a wasted land."[26] George remembers the
vicious mood of the times, with many dying in the mines and
others in labor violence—a shocking contrast to the parallel
universe of rural times portrayed so beautifully in both the
novel, and the movie, *A River Runs Through It*:

> My father was a sturdy Illinois farm hand, a semi-
> pro baseball player, Spanish-American War veteran,
> who worked in the hazardous depths of Butte's cop-
> per mines in order to feed and clothe his family. He
> escaped the violent death that befell many, but on
> a cold January night in 1919 he died as I held him
> in my arms while the remnants of his metal-laden
> lungs hemorrhaged out of his nose and mouth in
> an unceasing, unstoppable torrent of his life blood.
> My wife's own father was killed in an under-
> ground mine accident. These were truly hard times
> and death, in various guises, stalked the streets and
> entered the humble homes with great frequency.[27]

For George, then, fly fishing was not merely a way of life.
It was a way out of one way of life and into another. He was
not a strong child, so it is little surprise that he sought refuge
and pleasure along the Big Hole River south of Butte. The
Big Hole, he once wrote, is a river "such as one might expect
to find in Heaven—or be willing to go elsewhere in search
of."[28] It was there he developed his flies, and there he grew
to be one of Montana's staunchest angler-conservationists.

His passion for the river would eventually be essential to its survival as trout habitat.

Sadly, this most celebrated of fly weavers was never able to make a comfortable living from his trade. He worked in a variety of more "respectable" occupations, remembering that one of the best things that ever happened to him was in 1933 when he lost his job and started spending entire summers living in a small cabin along the Big Hole. Life seemed always to be a financial struggle, waged more successfully by his wife, Annabell, whom he proudly acknowledges supported him while he pursued his work. When he retired at age sixty-one he was well known in the area as a fly tier, but no more so than Pott had been in earlier times.

Then, when most men would be content to sit by their favorite river, he launched a career as a writer and fly-tying authority. In the early 1970s, his two books *Montana Trout Flies* and *The Art of Weaving Hair Hackles for Trout Flies*, appeared, both homegrown, self-published little volumes. Their appearance changed forever the fishing world's awareness of the craft of fly weaving. What had before been an arcane, little-appreciated method was now exposed to a whole new generation of anglers, at a time when fly tying was enjoying unprecedented popularity. In eight years, the books sold ten thousand copies, an extraordinary achievement for an isloated individual with no background in publishing, marketing, or distributing. Both were later expanded and brought out in handsome hardbound editions, titled *The Master Fly Weaver* (1980) and *Montana Trout Flies* (1981). Besides constituting the mother lode of information on

Grant's craft, the books were for many years the premier source for Montana fly-tying and fly-fishing history as well.

Thanks to the books, and to his increased opportunities to tie and display his flies before a growing fly-fishing community, honors began to pile up, and George's work was widely acclaimed by the sport's leading figures, including Dave Whitlock, Ernest Schwiebert, and Joe Bates. Now a recognized Montana institution, George was featured in the State of Montana's gorgeous film, *Three Men, Three Rivers,* which celebrated the lives and achievements of three historic anglers and the rivers they were associated with: George and the Big Hole, Bud Lilly and the Madison, and Dan Bailey and the Yellowstone.[29]

Grant also became a hero to Montana conservationists, working tirelessly for trout stream protection. For many years editor of Butte Trout Unlimited's newsletter, *The River Rat,* he was a formidable and feisty adversary of various management agencies, water development interests, and others who competed with fishermen and trout for the use of the state's waters. His conservationist career, like those of a number of other Montanans including Dan Bailey and Bud Lilly, reveals how deeply entwined fly fishing had become with other aspects of life and commerce in the state. Agriculture, logging, tourism, and sport were routinely in conflict over resource allocation, and Grant not only enlisted as a foot soldier in these battles, but also inspired the next generation of anglers to carry on the struggle.[30]

George picked up the finer points of the fly-weaving trade early and carried the sophistication of the procedures to

Under George Grant's editorship, The River Rat, *the homegrown newsletter of the Butte, Montana, chapter of Trout Unlimited, became a powerful voice for the advocacy of trout stream conservation, and in 1974 became the official publication of Montana Trout Unlimited, which it remained until the late 1970s.*

Courtesy Todd Collins and the George Grant Chapter,
Trout Unlimited, Butte, Montana

remarkable heights, eventually becoming nationally renowned in fly-tying circles. It was George, in fact, who looked back on the origins of woven-fly methods and pointed out that the names of Pott's most popular patterns, such as the Sandy Mite and the Lady Mite, were "derived from the word 'hellgrammite,' western vernacular for all large species of the stone fly nymph."[31]

Grant thought the mites worked so well partly because the fish were still fairly unsophisticated. No doubt that was true, but even though the flies were not in proportion or configuration all that similar to the salmonfly nymph, they were actually much more like the real insect than had been any of their predecessors among the eastern wet flies. The mites were, in fact, not generic wet flies at all; they were the first genuine western nymph patterns.

Grant's own first significant contribution was the Black Creeper, a heavy, segmented-bodied (wraps of black monofilament formed the segments) wet fly with stiff hair hackles that would stick out from the body in the heaviest of currents. He first tied the prototype in 1931 and established the final pattern in 1937, and it was as close as a trout could come at the time to seeing a salmonfly nymph imitation.

The Black Creeper, Grant's first important contribution to the fly-tying craft, was at the time of its introduction in the 1930s the most precise commercial imitation of a salmonfly nymph.

Courtesy Doug O'looney

George may be most famous for the flawless stone fly nymphs that descended from the Black Creeper, flies whose bodies were made with flat clear monofilament over a colored foundation; every fly tier does a double-take at first sight of these. Not, strictly speaking, woven-bodied at all, they still seem a firm part of the weaver's tradition and are themselves as distinct from conventional wet flies as the woven flies. I first saw them about thirty years ago in Bud Lilly's

Countless streams throughout the northern Rockies
feature good stone fly habitat, making imitation of these
insects the highest priority for generations of anglers.

Bill Browning, photographer, Montana Historical Society
Photograph Archives, Helena

shop in West Yellowstone. The flies were so freshly conceived, so perfectly formed, and so gripplingly seductive that if you saw them you simply had to buy a couple—though I'm sure that most of us who bought them had no intention of doing anything more risky with them than taking them out of their box and admiring them now and then. Grant achieved that peculiar stature as a fly tier that is both a blessing and a curse, of producing flies so good that people refuse to fish with them. (When this happened, he had the foresight to run with it, cranking out countless presentation sets of his flies to be sold for conservation fund-raising.)

The monofilament-bodied nymphs are only a small part of Grant's legacy. He produced numerous variations on the old Pott-style flies, incorporating a wider variety of hairs as well as monofilament. His dry flies, with their extraordinarily thick, bushy hackles, cannot be matched for floatability by any feather hackle. These dry flies are especially interesting because George is almost exclusively a large-nymph fisherman. "I don't use dry flies much," he told me when I visited him in Butte in the mid-1980s. "I never have. When I was developing these dry-fly hackles I fished almost all the time with them for a year or so, just to see how they worked." They worked, he discovered, just fine.

Among the most striking Grant creations, once one gets over the raw covetousness brought on by the dry flies, was a series of rough-bodied nymphs made from squirrel hair. The hair was woven into a long "hackle" that was wrapped up the shank of the hook over a lead-wire foundation that flared the hair at spiraling intervals. The effect was a ragged, segmented, and utterly buggy body.

Grant and his predecessors represent one of the most interesting movements in the entire quirky history of American fly fishing. And for all their originality, what may stand out most in their story is their remarkable success as fishermen using a type of fly that had no fashionable acceptance elsewhere. They divorced themselves from the mainstream of angling thought and found their own way, and they caught as many fish as anybody else. I have elsewhere written of the somewhat hidebound, conservative temperament that seemed to rule fly fishing for centuries; the Montana fly weavers demonstrated that fly fishing could, indeed, break free of its traditions (some would call them paradigms) and develop successful alternatives that were both personally satisfying and practically useful.

PROOF

In the past few decades, fly fishers have been caught up in a world of fuzzy nymphs, jointed body flies, flexible nymphs, and the like, all aimed at making the fly more realistic and acceptable to the trout. We are told, in many books and articles, that softness and fuzziness are essential, that a fly must wave and wiggle in the water, that trout can feel the hard body of a fly and will spit it out quicker than they would a more chewy fly. We are told, in short, that flies like those tied by Pott and Grant can't be good.

Let's set aside for a moment the proof—the tremendous catches the fly weavers made—and consider these flies in their context. We know they have faded from fashion even in Montana, but dealers tell me that's more a matter of their cost and the trend consciousness of younger anglers who want the latest patterns than a matter of the flies' effectiveness. It doesn't really explain what is good or bad about the flies.

The western rivers help to explain it. Most of the flies tied by Pott, Jack Boehme, Grant, and the rest were large, for use in heavy, swift water. Some may have inadvertently imitated stone fly nymphs, many just looked like something the trout wanted to eat. Things happen fast in these waters, and the fish have to decide instantly whether or not to eat a fly. They often hook themselves under such circumstances, which means they didn't have much opportunity to spit out the fly anyway. The stiff hair hackles of the woven flies stand out in anything from still water to a torrent, visible all the time.

It also seems unlikely that in such waters the texture of the fly is all that important. Those who emphasize the importance of a fly being chewy are assuming a great deal about a fish's perceptions. They are assuming, for one thing, that the fish will be more concerned about the fly's body than about the steel hook that protrudes from the fly's rear end or the leader that the fly dangles from. With these unnatural attachments, the fly is already pretty unlike the fish's normal food; fly-tying theorists who advocate chewy flies are apparently assuming the trout will be a good enough sport not to be bothered by the hook and the leader. The truth is, we don't know what the trout makes of a fly, hard body or soft. We only know what works.

More important, hard bodies are not necessarily unnatural. The nymph of the salmonfly looks almost armored at first glance. The fish not only tolerate hard-bodied nymphs, they may well be expecting them.

I remember asking George Grant about these criticisms of the woven-bodied flies. It was about the only time in our conversations that I ever saw him get openly impatient. "You know," he said, "when I first started to get known, people would look at my flies and laugh. They couldn't believe a fly that wasn't fuzzy would work, or they'd say, 'well, that's very pretty but I wouldn't want to fish with it, it's too nice,' or something like that." I winced, remembering the flies I'd bought just to admire, and he continued. "They don't know; they never tried the flies. When I was a younger man, there were some of us who fished the Big Hole hard, all year. We were pretty competitive, and I can't say I always caught the most fish, but I often did." Faded snapshots of magnificent brown trout stretched out in a row, dwarfing rulers, prove his point. Even if there is some question why, there is no doubt that the woven-hair flies work very well. They work well enough that, though they are no longer the staple for many Montana anglers, they are not likely to disappear, and they are still having their effect as new variations are developed. The weaving styles developed by Pott and the rest are being adapted to new flies made not of hair, but of wools, chenilles, and various synthetics.

COMPLICATED LEGACIES

It would make for a tidy conclusion to say that the Montana fly weavers were so independent because they were on a frontier of fly fishing; that they broke away from established traditions so easily and so successfully because they were free from the hidebound attitude that comes from fishing waters that have been fished for hundreds of years. There is something to that, but it isn't that simple. Dan Bailey brought from the East a profound awareness of American and European fly-tying traditions; he did not abandon them. He built on them. George Grant counts among those who most influenced his early work eastern and European authors such as Paul Young, Louis Rhead, and Major J. H. Hale. From this mixed legacy—the teachings of earlier generations and the challenges of new waters—Montana's master weavers created their own tradition. They knew that the old books and the old ideas were useful only to a point.

This brief travelogue through 120 years of salmonfly imitation convinces me of one of the ways that western fly fishing really has been different from eastern fly fishing. In the East, as in England, the early angling entomologies, especially those that were written after dry-fly fishing became the fashion in the late 1800s and early 1900s, were mostly about mayflies. Right or wrong, anglers placed mayflies at the center of their sport's focus. They discussed caddis flies, stone flies, and other types, but the mayfly was the supreme insect of fly fishing. The milestone angling entomologies produced by Preston Jennings, Art Flick, Ernest Schwiebert, and others in the 1930s, 1940s, and 1950s were most heavily invested in the older English tradition of imitating mayflies. Other types of insects were always there, but it was primarily a mayfly enterprise.

In the West, it went differently. Though, as modern anglers know, the West has many superb and prolific mayfly hatches, western fly tying was for many years disproportionately influenced by the need to imitate a different type of insect, and, in fact, one species—the salmonfly. Perhaps it happened this way in part because the East and the Midwest had already developed so many good mayfly patterns. But whatever the causes, western fly tiers were much more focused on the stone flies (and, later, the caddis flies) than had been their eastern counterparts.

This is clear in the work of the fly weavers. The Mites were generally not tied as large as the actual insect known as the salmonfly, but they captured the spirit of that fly. (Veteran Montana angler Bud Lilly tells me that in the 1930s, even when he and his friends were fly fishing, they used to catch one or two live salmonflies and impale them on their Mites, just to make sure.) The entire Bunyan Bug series is a testament to the effectiveness of the salmonfly silhouette; all the others in the series are just scaled-down versions of the real thing. More recently, Charlie Brooks's hefty Montana Stone is echoed in his smaller nymphs, again just reduced (but still hefty) versions of the big one.

One has the feeling that for several generations there, up until maybe the 1970s, western fly fishers weren't all that unlike me when I first discovered these big flies. At a given moment, they might have been fishing something else, but they were more or less always wondering if a salmonfly might work better.

Of course in the 1970s, at the dawn of the *Selective Trout* era, when comprehensive modern angling entomologies began to appear, many anglers left that simpler world behind.

Western fly fishers, even the stodgy among us, were quickly exposed to a whole host of fishing gear, methods, and opportunities that we had ignored, or at least neglected. The hatches got sorted out and imitated, and now a visit to a fly shop in the Rockies is a yearly re-education in a world of newly developed fly patterns.

Ironically, that's been a good thing for the salmonfly, too. Season after season, I can walk into my favorite fly shops and count on some thoughtful tier to have dreamed up yet another version of the salmonfly. It's become a tradition of my own, the anticipation of what's new in salmonflies. Between the ones I buy and the ones I tie, the spirit of invention that inspired Pott, Means, Grant, and all the rest is still alive for me.

A River Runs Through It, *first the book and then the movie,
were milestones in the creation of the modern image of
western fly fishing, with effects rippling out beyond the
customary world of fly fishing into real estate, advertising,
and rarified circles of popular criticism.*

CHAPTER SIX

A River Runs Through It as Folklore and History

Their only mistake was that some of them forgot that fly fishing is a pastime, not a religion, and that is the kind of mistake that anyone could make.

—Andrew Herd, *The Fly* (2003)

My friend Gordon Brittan, professor of philosophy at Montana State University, has aptly described *A River Runs Through It* as a "common text" for fishermen.[1] To my mind, this label is the most telling, and the most powerful, compliment a book could receive. To produce a book on any subject that reaches into so many hearts, and speaks to so many wildly dissimilar personalities, must be the finest dream of a writer:

> It is simply a fact, I think, that to the extent that we have read the same books, and by virtue of this shared experience or idea and expression, we can communicate more fully with one another, at the very least being able to presuppose common meanings and a wider range of associations.[2]

What I may like best about this line of reasoning is that merely because *A River Runs Through It* is one of our common texts in no way means that we will learn from it, enjoy it, or even judge its significance in common ways. For a community of readers, all it may mean is that the book gives us a bit of common ground to stand upon—or water to wade in—and that it is in some way powerful and important enough that we each take it quite personally.

It wouldn't matter in the slightest if I didn't share Gordon's assessment of this book as a masterpiece—a "classic," to use his word. Whatever approval or disapproval I may have of the book would have no measurable effect on the still-ascending arc of its literary glory. So even if I did have criticisms of it, I wouldn't bother to offer them here. I don't believe that the arc could be deflected yet. Time will tell us if our celebrations are justified. I assume they are.

On the other hand, if we can't really say much about the text, there is a great deal to be said about its readers. There is both instruction and fun to be had in having a look at how the reading of *A River Runs Through It* is going. For a common text, it has been blessed with some distinctly uncommon readers.

The designation of a "classic" is a complicated business, a kind of critical cottage industry of its own, full of loft and honor and wisdom on the one hand, and commerce and hype and bandwagon-hopping on the other. The formal reaction to *A River Runs Through It,* as with the commentary generated by any celebrated book, is in a way a kind of literary annex to the common text itself. In the long haul, most of it will be forgotten, but I do think it can push public perception of the book this way or that enough to make a difference in its future. If one cares enough about the original book, and feels a stake in its future, this is reason enough to want to monitor the commentary on it. So I will do that, and will start with my own reactions.

Fly fishers love heroes, which probably explains why we have so many of them. Our heroes are everywhere, and perhaps the most joyous thing about the sport is that at any moment any one of us might suddenly become one, if only in our own eyes. Even the most pedestrian instructional manuals on how to fly fish sustain murky implications of great accomplishment, as if it would only take the gentlest of nudges to elevate all this arid prose about fly-line weight and hackle quality directly up into the realm of Quest Literature. I recently read the advanced proofs of a fly-fishing novella that repeatedly claims that *God* is a fly fisher.

But, like pretty much everyone else, we fly fishers prefer our heroes—except God, I guess—flawed. Judging from the stories we tell and write, we love reprobates, poachers, iconoclasts, and other mildly sociopathic forms of humanity who have little in common except that they are really great at catching fish. Most of us don't have what it takes to become an authentic trout bum, but we hold such people in high esteem.

I recently gave a little talk about writing to the fifth- and sixth-graders at my local school. I showed them how books are made, told them some things about writing, and read them some things I really liked.

Then, when we were just sitting and talking, I asked them what they thought of Harry Potter. What had been a mildly enthusiastic audience went nuts, chattering all at once, filling me in on details not just about the books, but about the author. I had struck a great sensitive pre-adolescent nerve.

But I noticed that when I first asked which of them had read the Harry Potter books, one girl did not raise her hand, and she was quiet through the whole frenzy of conversation. Afterwards, when the group scattered but I was still standing around, I had a chance to ask her why.

I was worried that this might be a delicate question. I could sense that the situation distanced her a little from her classmates. Maybe her parents couldn't afford the books, or didn't like that kind of thing. But I'm glad I asked. I don't remember her exact words, but her answer was clear and simple. She explained, with obvious exasperation, that she didn't read the books because everyone else *was* reading them—because they were just so annoyingly fashionable.

I sympathized with her because I recognized the feeling. I had the same feeling once myself, when it seemed a social sin to not be reading a book that everyone was raving about, and I was damned if I was going to give in to that kind of pressure.

The book was *A River Runs Through It,* and it came along in 1976. I don't remember how long it took, but I suspect it was at least ten years before I read it, even though I was a constant, enthusiastic, and critical reader of books on fishing and nature.

Some willful resistance to fashion is a very good thing, but I *suspect* that I also found the book a little threatening. There I was, deep in my own awakening to the power of rivers and wildness, stirred by vague ambitions of making something literary of it all, and I could tell just from the perfection of his title that this Maclean chap had gone about more or less the same thing.

Why did I put off reading such a promising book? Maybe I didn't want to admit that he might have done it a lot better than I could. Maybe I was afraid he had done it so well I wouldn't even need to bother. More constructively, maybe I just didn't want his translation of the experience to muddle my own when I was still sorting mine out.

It was probably all of these things and others I still haven't thought of. But as I said, I finally got over it and read the book, and I had no trouble admitting that my friends, and the more astute literary critics, were right. This was great stuff.

I am not convinced that good literature *must* be troubling, but rarely has a work about fishing been as usefully troubling for me as Maclean's book. If I fail to effuse over the quality of the book, it's only because many others have so success-fully covered that ground. But if I learned anything during the year or so I spent as an undergraduate English major, it was that masterpieces are made to be picked at.

Actually, my first reading of the story was kind of a relief. No doubt to his further credit, Maclean clearly was not up to the same things I was. Most of all, he brought with him from his distinguished background in literary scholarship that fine and graciously tuned sense of hopelessness about life that is almost a requirement for important fiction. It only took me the first few pages to see past his pleasant reminiscence of learning to fish from his father—by the way, this is among the most time-worn clichés of outdoor writing, which Maclean somehow managed to revive and bring to such delightful life that one would not imagine hundreds of other writers had done it before him—as I say, it only took me those first few pages to know precisely where all this was going. There were some epically flawed heroes in action here, and we all know what happens to them. There might be some fun along the way, but someone was going to die unpleasantly before this story was over. It was, literally, written all over these people that at least one if not several of them were going to walk right into heart-wrenching unhappiness, the kind of classically trained misery we require from major literature.

The prelude to this darkness starts on page 2, when Maclean made this explanatory remark:

> As a Scot and a Presbyterian, my father believed that man by nature was a mess and had fallen from an original state of grace. Somehow, I early developed the notion that he had done this by falling from a tree.[3]

I find Pastor Maclean enormously intriguing. For me he is the most engaging character in the book. He doesn't show up enough to suit me. I can perhaps best justify this highly personal opinion with an explanatory remark about myself. As a German and a Lutheran, *my* father believed that man by nature needed a lot of work, but if we all stuck with it there was great hope that we could rise *back* to grace. Somehow, when my father stood in his pulpit and intoned, "Lord have mercy upon us," *I* early developed the notion that Mercy was a very large, ill-featured old man in a dark suit who would jump on us if we misbehaved. I didn't picture him jumping from a tree, though. (I also wonder where I got the part about the dark suit.)

It seems to me both odd and revealing that these two men—Pastor Maclean and Pastor Schullery—from equally stern and demanding backgrounds, should exercise their faiths so heartily, and to the advantage of so many people, but with such contrasting visions of what they're about. But, just as I am sure that Norman Maclean preferred his father's vision, so do I prefer mine.

But none of this is about the book; it is about my reaction to the book. And it was immediately plain to me that the public liked all this darkness. I came to recognize *A River Runs Through It* as a key force in the rise of an intriguing new regional literary form I have come to think of as "Big Sky Angst." These are fishing stories in which educated, healthy, well-fed white people live in one of the most beautiful places on earth, do a fair amount of fly fishing on transcendantly lovely rivers, and are, of course, miserable.

Maclean's novel resonated with another of my cynicisms about serious literature, the overwhelming urge of the critical reader to proclaim what a book was actually "about." I remembered this sort of literary vivisection from college, where it was well known that no important work of fiction has ever been about the story it tells.

I always thought this decoding exercise was pretty hard on readers. It places unreasonable demands on them when the odds are strong that all they want is to read a good story. But Maclean himself said that *A River Runs Through It,* "despite all the talk so far about fishing, is not really a fishing story."

Right. For all the fanfare the book received from the fly-fishing community, we do need to admit this. *A River Runs Through It* is about other things, even though people do fish here and there in the story. But I also think that the story wouldn't work—and the book would not have become either successful or fashionable—if he had somehow written it without the fishing. And thank heavens, it is without question true that just as you can happily and rightly read *Gulliver's Travels* or *Huckleberry Finn* solely as adventure tales, you *can* read *A River Runs Through It* as a fishing story, whatever higher calling it may have had for the author or for all the symbolism and portent revealed in the critical autopsies we keep performing on it.

This multi-level, allegory-scavenging business is central to the literary enterprise, and it has a peculiar importance to lovers of fishing books. For generations, we've prided ourselves on the cultural richness of what we do. We love it when a Hemingway, a Maclean, or a McGuane comes along and gives our little sport the boost in tone that invariably attaches to us from such eminent attentions. Fly fishing's modest literary establishment may never recover from those heady days in the 1960s and 1970s, when Arnold Gingrich, founder of *Esquire* magazine and companion of all the literary giants of his time, became the sport's foremost commentator. We love this kind of stuff.

I think Maclean loved it too, which proves how much he loved fly fishing. His book is full of the sort of self-elevating rhetoric that would have guaranteed its popularity among fly fishers even if the literary snoots had panned it. For example, like many writers before him, Maclean described fishing as an art. In other writings, he used the same term almost relentlessly, not only to describe fly fishing but also horse packing, baseball, teaching, and logging. They were all arts to him. He knew what he meant, and he rationalized it well, but in any formal, defensible sense of these words, with the possible exception of teaching, they are not arts.

But it's a really easy sell, isn't it? Even Wallace Stegner succumbed to these seductive sentiments on our behalf, telling us that "fishing with a dry fly, which is the skill that gives both meaning and form to *A River Runs Through It,* is not a labor but an art, not an occupation but a passion, not a mere

Norman Maclean, *woodcut by James G. Todd Jr.*

Courtesy the artist

skill but a mystery, a symbolic reflection of life."[4] Well, fine. Sounds just like the way other enthusiasts feel about canoeing, collecting beer cans, and hacking the Web. Let's *all* be artists.

This enthusiastic buying into the book's message, of angling as art, even though it is mostly done by critics with no known familiarity with fly fishing or its literature, is yet another testament to the strength of what Maclean achieved. There is in *A River Runs Through It* a consistent and admirably expressed sense of the greater importance of certain actions, especially things done by hand or with tools that take some mastering and demand passion. If we're at all serious about fishing, passion is not a strange word to us. For Maclean, and for most of us as we fish, there is no instant in a day's fishing that cannot suddenly become momentous. It's powerful stuff we're doing out there.

This power has swept away some other momentous commentators, too. According to Wendell Berry's interpretation of the book, "fly fishing is seen, then, as a way of recovering God's rhythms and attaining grace."[5]

There's God again. I can't speak for Pastor Maclean, of course, and such a question would probably never have occurred to Pastor Schullery, but I suspect that either of these professional Protestants, if confronted with Berry's statement, might wonder if it isn't at least mildly blasphemous. They might not have a lot of use for the airs we tend to put on as we seek to understand Maclean's book. The fictional Pastor Maclean is neither my literary creation nor my father, but I think I can safely imagine him wondering aloud at all this enthusiasm for the eternal verities and descriptive felicities of the book's fishing scenes, being expressed by people who don't even fish themselves. Are they perhaps a little too caught up in the newly revealed intellectual hipness of the sport?

But let's not lose sight of something astonishing that is happening here. Remember that in the general social view of the past several centuries the very act of fishing has been most widely perceived as a kind of tragic vice itself, a wastrel's pastime—the anti-social recreation of unrepentant, overgrown boys. I wonder if perhaps the greatest achievement of Maclean's book isn't in how beautifully he told of the fly-fishing life—many have written as eloquently about the sport as he did—or even in what he did for the regional real estate market. It might be that, unlike so many others, he took fishing—or at least one specific kind of fishing—and raised it from several centuries of social and intellectual marginalizing, making it something the Stegners and Berrys could relate to.

This sounds like a good thing, but as I've suggested earlier in this book, it has its risks. Maclean succeeded in inviting the attention of a lot of cool hands from other academic disciplines into an intellectual arena that may be ill prepared for such scrutiny. Are we fly fishers really ready for this?

And a more important question comes to mind when I read what these higher minds have written about fly fishing. I wonder: Are *they* ready for it? For all their learning and distinction, some of these critics seem to be pretty easily suckered into simplistic views of what's going on in fly fishing.

Consider, for example, the most tragic character of *A River Runs Through It,* Paul Maclean. Maclean stated and plainly believed that his brother was one of the finest, if not the finest, fly fisher in the Northwest. For the purposes of the fictional brother in his novel, that is a reasonably defensible characterization. You want this guy to be really great at catching fish for the story to work best.

But in the criticism I have read, especially as that criticism is conducted by famously literate non-anglers, I see this characterization taking on the rigor of history. Here, the claim becomes shaky and worrisome. If you've fished much you know that in any rural community with a lot of water around, there are going to be Paul Macleans. Most of them we will never hear of, but remember that at the time of the final fishing trip of Norman, Paul, and Pastor Maclean, there in western Montana, George Grant and his pals were engaged just as fiercely in fishing the Big Hole, and a father and son both named Walen Lilly were hoovering up trout on the Madison and Gallatin. Montana, Idaho, Colorado, and the rest of the West was no doubt likewise generating local masters like these. It is no insult to their skills to point out that every town and every river has these amazing fishermen. Who is to say that one is the best?

Which raises a more important question, one that just begs for attention throughout any careful reading of *A River Runs Through It,* but one that is utterly lost on the outsider-commentators who have chosen to dabble in literary criticism of this book—What is a great fisherman anyway? Even a brief acquaintance with the codes and traditions of fly fishing will suggest that the Paul Maclean of *A River Runs Through It* is a dubious candidate for the title. If this is a sport (much less if it's an art) there is lot more going on than mere production of dead fish. And here our literary giants, newcomers to the complex and not easily acquired finer points of angling tradition, are most at risk of stumbling over their confidence.

Fishing culture isn't simple. The dominant literary strain for the past four centuries or so is based on a few books published in the fifteenth, sixteenth, and seventeenth centuries, by far the most distinguished of which was Izaak Walton's classic of didacticism and rural charm, *The Compleat Angler* (1653, though the final edition published during his life, in 1676, is generally regarded as the most *completely* compleat). Waltonian gentleness ("Study to be quiet") may be the most honored,

The "River" of Maclean's masterpiece is Montana's Big Blackfoot, shown here at its confluence with the Clearwater in the 1890s.

Myrta Wright Stephens, photographer,
Montana Historical Society Photograph Archives, Helena

repeated, and widely recognized element of the angling tradition, but it's hardly the only way to go. Several modern writers have displayed and championed significant variants on the angler's lifeway. The late Lee Wulff, among the most highly honored anglers of the last century, brought an almost Olympic athleticism to the sport. Ernest Schwiebert, like Wulff one of the giant figures of the past century for his contributions to angling practice and theory, probably did more than anyone else to celebrate and honor the sport's cosmopolitan scope. Arnold Gingrich found in the sport endless opportunities for satisfying, gossipy inquiry. Gary Lafontaine was a joyous empirical overachiever, attacking angling problems that most of us just tolerate, with a scientific passion for technical improvement. There are apparently many kinds of great fishermen, and we need to be open-minded about these definitions.

Still, I'm hard pressed to find angling greatness in Paul Maclean. In the words of the fictional Maclean boys, it was simply true that the number of bastards increases rapidly the farther one gets from Missoula, Montana. This was as straightforward a bioregional code as you are likely to find. In fact, I have wondered if Maclean himself realized the extent to which his book demonstrated the universality of bastardhood in the characterization of his hero angler, Paul. Paul is, I suspect, an even more tragic figure than his family realized. I sympathize with all the good souls in the book who are helpless in the face of Paul's self-destructive addictions to alcohol, gambling, and violence, but, lacking the family bond that warms the heart, I still take a colder view. Paul looks to me to be a pretty thorough bastard right there *in* Missoula, Montana.

Even more important, he is obviously not someone I would ever want to fish with. It is no surprise; in fact, it is perfect that Maclean portrays Paul as rejecting Izaak Walton. Paul is a pie in the face of every Waltonian principle.

Set aside for a moment that Paul enjoys beating up men and women, though of course that's not the sort of thing one could casually set aside in choosing one's companions. What kind of fisherman is he? Well, he's a showoff. He's a lousy sport who will spoil another fisherman's spot rather than be outfished. He is ferociously competitive, using fly fishing to confirm his superiority over all the other bastards. When he goes fishing, he likes a bet on the side. As Maclean once said about his brother in an interview, "Fishing for him was an elegant sport and all that, but essentially fishing was getting fish and beating the other guy. Anything to beat him!"

This isn't just a matter of his rivalries with other anglers. His relationship *with the river itself* seems so hostile and adversarial that he might as well be exercising an angry grudge in some beer-hall bowling tournament. This problem of Paul's—his employment of this gentle sport for such raw, violent ends—is for me one of the least savory things that the river runs through. Anyone who could think of fly fishing dismissively as "an elegant sport and all that" doesn't even make my list of people I want on the same river with me. No amount of technical proficiency, even brilliance, at catching fish can make me think such a person would be a tolerable fishing companion. Pastor Maclean sounds like a lot more fun.

(By the way, I don't think we can rescue some distinction for Paul Maclean by claiming that he is a uniquely new kind of fisherman, a product of the raw western frontier. He may be such a product, but it doesn't make him unique. By all accounts, there have been jerks fishing trout streams as long as there have been trout streams. His lack of sportsmanship has no regional distinctiveness to it; its like has gone on for centuries.)

So I suspect we would be doing good work if we caution the newcomer to fly-fishing literature not to assume that Paul Maclean is some kind of polished archetype of the great angler.

The flurry of criticism and analysis of *A River Runs Through It* contains other tendencies that we probably need to watch for. In a lecture, Maclean himself quoted a prominent and admiring fisherman as saying that "There are hundreds of books and articles on how to fly fish, but only Maclean tells you how it feels."[6] Now, in this greater world of which fly fishing is becoming a more respected part, a remark like that can quickly take on unseemly authority, though in fact it is nearly illiterate. I worry that non-angling literary scholars will tend to buy such a claim and feel no obligation to check it—to discover Walton, much less Roderick Haig-Brown, or Thaddeus Norris, or George Edward McKenzie Skues, or Harry Middleton, or Odell Shepard, or any of the hundreds of others who have quite ably celebrated what fly fishing feels like.

Here is where we who fish, and who like to think of ourselves as fairly familiar with the sport's literary and intellectual foundations, should pay attention to what's going on among the new fly-fishing readers. The legitimizing of angling writing and criticism as a respectable intellectual pursuit brings certain obligations to the intellectuals. I hope they're ready, and that we're ready to help them find their way.

At the same time that I advise caution in all these things, I find *A River Runs Through It* to be full of revealing history. Norman's first sight of the Bunyan Bug, which I have mentioned already on page 142, preserves for us one of those precious little moments of insight and discovery that always enrich fly fishing. I don't doubt that many of us who have put in a few years have had the very same experience when introduced to some meaningfully different kind of fly: we took one look at it and felt perfect. When McClean says that, we know just what he means, and we know we're looking in on such a moment in fly fishing's history.[7] As noted in the previous chapter, the distinctive fly patterns that were developed in relative aesthetic isolation in the northern Rockies eighty years ago still stand out as among the most curious and stimulating directions the craft of fly tying has yet taken in the New World. McClean captured that for us, in a few sentences.

Even more impressive is Maclean's portrayal of Paul's evolution as a technically proficient fly caster. You will recall how Paul goes from being his father's understudy to being something far more, something never imagined by Pastor Maclean's generation of anglers. What Maclean achieves here is no less than contrasting the universal but somewhat confining casting style of virtually all nineteenth-century fly fishers with the rise of a far more open, free-wheeling style of casting whose development in early-twentieth-century fly fishing did indeed pretty much coincide with the years of Paul's fishing career. By the way, I also thought that Robert Redford's depiction of this contrast in the movie was superb. There *is* history in this book, and it is unusually vivid.

A River Runs Through It serves as a warm invitation to academics to move into an exciting and relatively unconsidered field of writing and thinking. My little ruminations on that book are just a hint of the questions we have facing us, and the endless inquiries that await us.

We are lucky beyond saying that Norman Maclean wrote this book, and that it found such a large and appreciative audience. Thanks in good part to *A River Runs Through It,* some very bright people have discovered what some of us knew all along—that fly fishing is indeed something special, and that it has inspired some wonderful writing. These very bright people have a lot to offer fly fishing. Now that we have their attention, we have a great deal more work to do.

*Charles Belden produced this promotional photograph
of Annice Williston Belden playing a trout in
Wyoming's Greybull River in the early 1900s.*

American Heritage Center, University of Wyoming, Laramie

CHAPTER SEVEN

Cowboy Trout

For more than a century the American West has been the most strongly imagined section of the United States.

—Richard White, *"It's Your Misfortune and None of My Own": A New History of the American West* (1991)

This book has had a lot to do with the dynamic nature of a sport—how it changes and how complicated it is to participate in a vital tradition whose adherents are both loyal to, and rebellious against, the ways of their ancestors. In my own thinking and writing, I seem most often to have considered this process of change from the perspective of centuries, but sometimes the changes happen much faster. As my years as a fly fisher become decades, I am shocked to realize that they have even happened to me.

The odds aren't good, but perhaps you have been fly fishing long enough to remember the Formal Times, when the sport was portrayed and taught as a much more standardized exercise than it is today. There were certain correct ways to cast (one, two, three . . . one, two, three—ten o-clock, one o-clock . . . ten o'clock, one o'clock), certain correct ways to tie flies, and certain correct ways to do pretty much everything else, including think. If you did things differently, you could almost count on someone wandering by and telling you about it.

The Formal Times ended, as near as I can remember, about the time of the resignation of Richard Nixon, in 1974 (not that I blame him; I assume this was a coincidence). One day right about then, on the Madison River, I had just landed a passable but not braggable rainbow when another fisherman, an older fellow whose entire costume said "Old School Fly," came by. When he asked what I'd caught the fish on, I proudly showed him my immense, home-tied green chenille stone fly nymph. (For some reason, perhaps because it is an accurate memory, when I recall that fly I think of it as tied on a heavy, stainless-steel saltwater hook, which would have made it all the more offensive.)

Such a fly, because of its relative bigness and crudeness, amounted to a violation of traditional fly-tying and fly-fishing aesthetics. There were at that time a good many older anglers who did not regard a pattern that big and heavy as even meeting the minimum definition of a fly. Apparently this fellow agreed. He sputtered indignantly at this brutish assault on the river and his refined sensitivities, then harumphed off downstream into the comfortingly self-righteous oblivion reserved for all those left behind in changing times. Ironically, at the time I'm sure that he would have thought I was the "drop-out"—the barber-deprived, flannel-shirted radical who couldn't handle the rules and was rebelling against the sensible terms of *real* fly fishing—but in the long haul it turned out that the sport was abandoning him, not me.

Since then, fly fishing has experienced an amazing flourishing of open-mindedness. Tradition has been replaced as the sport's watchword by a near-obsession for innovation and unorthodoxy. Fewer and fewer of us are old enough to remember what it was like before. Even fewer are inclined (like aging subversives on a park bench) to look back and wonder if the revolution was such a good idea after all. But it's here, and we continue to learn from it

As I suggested earlier in this book, changes like these have occurred for a long time. But they used to happen more slowly. A typical British fly fisher in 1700 would have used about the same tackle and techniques as had his ancestors in 1500, or 1300. The rate of change has accelerated in the past two centuries, probably because society has also changed at a much more rapid pace than ever before. Especially since the time of the American Civil War, each generation of anglers has given their technology, and even their attitudes, a good working over. Look how quickly we (at least many of us) went from defining a successful "fight" with a rainbow trout only in terms of how many jumps we got out of the fish to being more concerned with how fast we were able to land it and release it before it was exhausted. We still like the jumps, but now we think about what they cost. Some day we may even stop liking the jumps; they already worry me.

Nowhere is this process of reconsideration producing more restlessness, and revealing more about us, than in the conservation of native fish species, which, like so many other things that have to do with fly fishing, provide a helpful window into the past and prospects of the American West.

Cowboys and Native Americans

The notion of nativeness is one of the most engaging elements in our idea of the West. So much of what Americans, indeed people around the planet, think of as quintessentially western—as forming the foundation of our idea of the American West—is in fact problematic. In our imagined West, we have incorporated a great many visual props that grate against even the most elastic notions of authenticity.

For an example, let's consider the most popular exemplar of the "Old West"—the cowboy. The cowboy has suffered hard times at the hands of modern revisionists. He has become a great symbol of the complications of the West, belittled, demythologized, and dismissed by writers as diverse as Edward Abbey and Wallace Stegner, and though I recognize the wisdom of these critics, it still saddens me. I grew up watching Hopalong Cassidy and Roy Rogers and have never really escaped the cowboy enchantment.

But there is no denying that the cowboy and his employers have taken a heavy toll on the wildness of the West. Cowboys ride one exotic species in order to herd another exotic species to pastures where they feed on yet other exotic species. The effects of these sweeping intrusions on the native ecosystem were phenomenal, and if you were a native grazer that fed on native plants, or a native predator that fed on native grazers, you were out of luck and out of time. If the guns, traps, exotic livestock diseases, and fences didn't get you, eventually the settlement of your ancient migration routes just eliminated your world. Say it ain't so, Hoppy!

Only the first generation or two of western fly fishers relied solely on native fish for their sport. One example is this day's catch of Snake River finespotted cutthroat trout, taken from the Gros Ventre River of northwestern Wyoming by President Chester Arthur during his famous 1883 western tour.

F. Jay Haynes, photographer, Haynes Foundation Collection,
Montana Historical Society Photograph Archives, Helena

And yet the successful transplantation of this Old World animal husbandry industry to the New World has had immense popular appeal. It is an epic tale. It involved great heroism, innovation, and adaptation. It was hard work almost beyond comprehension. It was a continental-scale human adventure, played out against the spectacular backdrop of the western cordillera. It also involved breathtaking ignorance of ecological realities and the brutal crushing of native cultural systems, but I'm trying to stick to one set of issues here, so we'll let that go for now. For our immediate purposes, it is enough to say that the cowboy saga, as profoundly romantic as it was to us, brought about a dramatic and wholesale change in the native landscape. A once-wild West was replaced by the familiar, colorful, stereotypical Old West. Or, to put it another way, the Old West may have been wild, but it was the people, not the setting, that displayed the wildness.

So when a visiting angler looks from his drift boat, sees a cowboy riding a fenceline, and succumbs to the boyhood thrill of that glimpse of an earlier time, he is indeed seeing an older West. It is not in any sense an Original West, but it is a nice, tidy snapshot of a specific Previous West. It's just been sold to all of us as the Real West—as the West with enduring values and heroics against which to measure all subsequent Wests, and beside which all earlier Wests are ignored.

Of course, cowboys weren't the first people to affect the western landscape. The pre-Columbian West was not divorced from human influences, any more than it was immune to tremendous changes in plant and animal communities due to climatic variation. For ten or more millennia, Native Americans in sizeable if still hotly debated numbers were having all manner of likewise hotly debated effects on these same landscapes, including, for at least a couple thousand years prior to the arrival of Lewis and Clark, the use of fire to reshape various settings to suit their needs.[1]

So what happened when whites got here wasn't absolutely new. People had been tinkering with the scene for a long time.

What happened when whites got here was just an explosive, technologically abetted acceleration of the process. Tinkering became engineering. Engineering became massive overhauling. Nobody argues that this acceleration occurred, but everybody argues over what it means, and whether it's good or bad.

RESHAPING AQUATIC ECOSYSTEMS
JUST SOMETHING ELSE WE DO

What happened in the West happened quite literally all over the world. Humans, in many places they have lived, have long tinkered locally with their fish populations. Our best documentation for this process may come from medieval Europe, where increasing market demands for fish as food led to amazing changes in fish populations.

The spread of Christianity, interestingly, heightened these demands. As historian Richard Hoffmann, the most influential modern scholar of the origins of fly fishing, has pointed out, "Early Christians had avoided meat on ascetic and penitential grounds, which, refracted through the monastic practices of the early medieval church, became a general obligation of believers to abstain from eating the flesh of terrestrial quadrupeds about 150 days of the year."[2] The demand for fish as an alternative to mammal meat grew apace with the human population, and as those appetites were satisfied, the inhabitants of native ecosystems were drained into the markets and cook pots of eager consumers.

Hoffmann's synthesis of archeological records from numerous sites in Europe tracks the disappearance of preferred fish species from local diets. The disappearance of these species led to their replacement by less preferred species, by the rise of extensive fish culture and fish translocation, and by the resultant redistribution of formerly non-native fish species in new waters across Europe. Carp, for example, were confined to the Danube drainage in eastern Europe as late as 600 A.D., but over the course of the next nine hundred or so years, they moved progressively westward, reaching not only France, Germany, Scandinavia, and Poland, but also England.[3] This may seem a slow change by modern standards, but anybody who has seen carp make themselves at home in a local lake knows it was a momentous one. The process resulted in a comprehensive transformation:

> What would become traditional European techniques of fish farming combined systems of waterworks first visible in French sources of the twelfth century with the propagation of a fast-growing exotic pond fish from central Europe, the common carp. This aquatic "agroecosystem" took form between the Seine and the Rhine by the 1250s and by 1500 had spread across the continent. Artificial rearing supplied nearby elite markets for fresh fish throughout late medieval and early modern inland Europe. Because feral carp and related pond fishes were especially adapted to the warmer, slower,

weedier waters which economic growth was causing, they magnified change in the ecosystem.[4]

So centuries before things got stirred up in the American
West, Europeans had developed formidable skills at removing or sweeping aside native species. Even with the relatively
primitive tools of their time, they had a long reach.

That reach did not change significantly until almost yesterday. If you lived in 1800, your wagon full of fresh fish,
salted fish, or live fish could only move about as fast as had
your ancestor's wagon a thousand years earlier. But the
Industrial Revolution's suite of technological advances accelerated everything, except an eye for long-term consequences.
Thanks to steam, the great colonial powers suddenly had the
wherewithal to transform the biological communities of
their colonies and properties anywhere on the globe. It seemed
like the best possible thing to do, so they did it.

This isn't the place for a detailed discussion of what historian Alfred Crosby has called "ecological imperialism," beyond
pointing out that what happened was incredibly complex,
from the European social and cultural conditions that generated such a terrifically effective group of plant and animal
"imperialists" to the global conditions that set the stage for
this epic of conquest.[5] Beyond that obligatory stage-setting, I
want to turn to a few species that barely rate mention in the
scholarly books on the story of biological invasions—trout.
Trout, as central as they may seem in the lives of quite a few
westerners, were in effect just caught in the prop wash of this
much greater and more momentous process.

HOMESICK ANGLERS

The "acclimatization society" might serve as the symbol of the well-intended alteration of the earth's life communities. Starting with the Société d'Acclimatation, established in Paris in 1854, there rose a host of European and colonial groups whose goal was to translocate whatever assortment of domestic or wild species of plants and animals was deemed best, from wherever they lived to wherever they were needed.[6]

At first glance, there is without question something charming about what these people were doing. One pictures some glum British gents wandering through an Australian (or South American or African) meadow, until one of them suddenly brightens and announces, "I say, chaps, all this place really needs is a trout stream!"

And there does seem to have been a fair amount of that sort of homesickness prevention involved. Arthur Nicols, in *The Acclimisation of the Salmonidae at the Antipodes, Its History and Results* (1882), looked at the landscapes of Australia and New Zealand and reveled in dreams of "stalking the red deer and bringing the lordly salmon to grass among picturesque granitic hills, which may well recall to the eye of the sportsman many a wild scene in the highlands of Scotland or the softer glories of the Irish Lakes."[7] British angler J. C. Mottram, author of the insightful *Fly-Fishing: Some New Arts and Mysteries* (1915), wrote lovingly of fishing New Zealand and the unique sporting joys of mixing the exotic and the familiar in such places. Listing many of the strange bird songs heard along the trout streams of these new lands, he concluded that "For these things I am sure you would go ashore at Tasmania, to enjoy this new and strange accompaniment to our dear old song."[8]

But what the acclimatization societies had in mind was a lot broader than merely bringing the comforts of home to forlorn sportsmen. They would haul in any species with commercial or sporting or ornamental potential. "Say, why don't we give ostrich a try in the south pasture? The zebras don't seem to be doing all that well there anyway." As one British official summed it up in East Africa, "What white settlers will want to find here is wheat in their fields and trout in their rivers."[9]

And so it happened, perhaps even beyond the dreams of the original acclimatizers. Some of their organizations endured and were eventually transformed into early game management agencies. Others just faded away. The title of historian Thomas R. Dunlap's book, *The English Diaspora* (1999), like Crosby's earlier-mentioned book, suggests the magnitude of this movement, as does Dunlap in discussing these societies:

> Within a generation the fad had passed, but seldom have so few done so much over so large an area with so little effort (or understanding). Now there are English skylarks in Tasmanian fields, European rabbits across Australia and in New Zealand, and red deer in New Zealand's forests. Across North America English sparrows fight in the gutters and starling squabble in the trees. Everywhere the shock waves from these silent biological explosions continue to reverberate.[10]

Trout were an especially exciting and challenging part of this explosion. Unlike terrestrial mammals and birds, which could just be loaded on a ship and hauled pretty much anywhere, fish were hard to transport. The shipping system had to preserve and precisely chill delicate ova for a voyage of weeks or months, often through torrid climatic zones. There is a genuine sense of adventure and triumph in the accounts of those first attempts at transoceanic relocation of trout and salmon, especially in the immense journeys from England to Australasia (being troutless, this region attracted the attention of the transplanters well before North America did). Because of the experimentation involved—both technological, in developing the means of transport, and biological, in seeing if these species could thrive so far from home—the adventure was also a scientific one.[11]

The first attempt to bring salmonid ova to Australia occurred in 1852, and failed, as did subsequent attempts, but only by narrow circumstantial margins that did not discourage the determined acclimatizers. By 1864, methods for keeping the ova cool and fresh were perfected, and trout and salmon arrived in Australia and Tasmania. Very soon thereafter, anglers were raving about the great fishing—a common refrain, it appears, in regions where trout are introduced in ripe habitats, as their populations irrupt and provide spectacular fishing to the relatively few anglers around to enjoy them.

PLANET TROUT

Thus began the most remarkable era, and the most far-reaching change, in the world of trout fishing. Today, if we think about this spread of trout at all, we probably think of it as a fairly minor effort that targeted a few likely waters in a few likely countries, but what has been achieved is far grander than that. Canadian biologist Hugh MacCrimmon and his colleagues, in a series of nearly encyclopedic articles written in the late 1960s and early 1970s, documented the spread of trout around the world during the previous century, concluding that in the case of the browns and rainbows, there were now surprisingly few regional habitats left unoccupied: "Dissemination of the European brown trout appears to have been so complete in the past 100 years that most areas of the world capable of supporting significant natural populations have now received introductions."[12] The rainbow is, if anything, even more comprehensively distributed.

This isn't to say that there aren't many more waters where these fish could live or thrive; only that the gross distribution has been accomplished and what remains is local fleshing out of occupancy. That the trout-raising and trout-fishing industries had the persistence and clout to achieve this comprehensive level of success says a lot about both the commerce of trout and the demand for sport.

The planet-wide distribution process has had its interesting twists. A nineteenth-century fisheries manager who received one of those precious early shipments of brown trout from far-off Europe or rainbow trout from North America knew better than to summarily dump the lot into the nearest river and call it a victory. Local hatcheries were established everywhere and soon were themselves the source of additional regional or long-distance movements of the descendants of

A Montana Fish and Game (now Fish, Wildlife and Parks)
transplant truck stands ready to distribute another load of
trout to some needful water in the state in June 1950.

Montana Historical Society Photograph Archives, Helena

those same fish. It was an ecological chain letter of extreme
elegance and coverage.

A striking example of how this ricochet redistribution
worked is provided by Africa. By the time that MacCrimmon
and his colleagues published their summaries, more than
twenty African nations had either naturally reproducing or
artificially maintained rainbow trout populations. But not
one of those populations originated in a direct shipment
from North America, the rainbow's home continent. They
came via intermediate, generational stops at hatcheries as
far-flung as Scotland, Madagascar, Germany, Switzerland,
England, Portugal, and several African colonies that had
received earlier shipments.[13]

As an aside, it is worth pointing out that this trout dispersal, as disorderly, rushed, and mindless as it was, has functioned in some useful ways as a kind of unintentional scientific experiment. The huge success of the rainbow, the only modestly less complete success of the brown, the considerably more circumscribed success of the brook, and the general non-success of the cutthroat, when moved beyond their native ranges, have taught us many things about those species, their flexibility, and their biological needs. Of course there would have been a lot of less harmful ways of learning the same things.

But we now have a trout-rich, or trout-friendly, or trout-infested world. You can fish for them in an astonishing array of landscapes, to even more "strange and new accompaniments" than Mottram imagined almost a century ago. A hefty travel industry will take you there, and knowledgeable local guides will demystify the relevant insect hatches and, if necessary, ward off whatever large native predators might still pose a risk to the sportsman. The creation of Planet Trout is, by many accounts, a great success story, and by many other accounts, an unmitigated ecological disaster. And it has, by any account, caused big changes in the American West.

Controversy over non-native trout in the West is just a minor element in a far larger public dialogue over the loss of native species. Native species conservation and non-native species control are both growth industries, and no doubt will be for years to come as we attempt to deal with what science journalist Yvonne Baskin has called "a massive game of musical chairs we have played with life on earth."[14]

When it comes to aquatic species, trout actually occupy

the glamorous end of the spectrum of public interest and don't even offer the most striking examples of the changes underway. The survival of many native aquatic species are a hot topic in conservation circles in North America. Humans have already "caused the extinction of 40 taxa of North American fishes: 27 species, and 13 subspecies (as well as 3 genera) have been lost."[15] Two-thirds of the native mussel species, half of the crayfish species, and 40 percent of the fish and amphibians are in serious jeopardy.[16]

As for the trout, the eastern brook trout is for the most part holding on only in the headwaters of many of its native streams, most of which are now occupied by browns and rainbows. In an act of almost violent irony, while displacing brook trout from much of their native range, we have introduced them in countless other places on top of native species, thus making them instruments of further destruction of native ecosystems. Because of the readiness with which they stunt, their widespread distribution in my own home waters of Yellowstone Park have been to the advantage of relatively few anglers, most of whom want to catch bigger fish even if they don't care whether or not the fish is native.[17]

Much of this fish-translocation story has the grimness of many other environmental litanies of loss. In the Midwest, the Michigan grayling is gone. Farther west, the arctic grayling is down to about 8 percent of its historic range in the Lower Forty-Eight.[18] The Yellowstone cutthroat occupies only ten percent of its original stream range and is now struggling against new invaders, both fish and disease, in those diminished strongholds.[19] The westslope cutthroat, lacking the

*A fly fisher on Montana's Big Hole River admires a handsome
brook trout, native of the Appalachians.*

Bill Browning, photographer, Montana Historical Society
Photograph Archives, Helena

Yellowstone cutthroat's slightly more secure lake populations, is even more threatened. It might occupy a quarter of
its historic stream range, but it shares that range with other
species—introduced rainbows and other cutthroats—that
pose a dire threat to what remains of its genetic distinctiveness. Genetically pure populations occupy less than 3 percent
of the historic range of this species.[20]

Throughout the West, many other less famous but equally beautiful and distinctive trout populations have either already winked out or have achieved the tragic poster-child stage of nearly doing so. Anyone who listens to a few ecologists recite this tale of woe is inclined to agree with writer David Quammen (not generally known as an alarmist) that, in the world's modern catastrophic binge of species loss, "we're headed into another mass extinction, a vale of biological impoverishment."[21]

And it isn't surprising that the exchange of fish species from here to there and back again in North America, like so many other trades and transfers between the East and the West, has not been an even one. A survey of introductions revealed that "The predominant pattern has been introduction of species native to the eastern United States into western states, primarily in association with angling. Of the 17 most widely introduced species, 12 fit this category. . . . By contrast, only one western fish (rainbow trout) has been widely introduced into eastern states."[22] The West's relatively low fish diversity was seen from the beginning of settlement as a disadvantage; like the English gent in New Zealand, the eastern settler in the West knew how to bring his old home along with him.

BACKLASH

Native trout have always had a few defenders, east and west. Lifelong brook trout advocate Charles Lose, writing in *The Vanishing Trout* (1931), railed against "that shark of the trout streams, the brown trout—the trout that has scales, is stale in three hours after he is caught, feeds at night when honest anglers are in bed, and will eat his own grandmother if he can catch her."[23] Lose's hostility against the brown was almost matched by his hopefulness that the native brook trout could be restored. But from the late 1800s on, most anglers were as hopeless about bringing back the native fish as were the few people who mourned the destruction of the bison herds—we lost them, too bad, nothing we can do about it.

That fatalistic pessimism no longer prevails. In the past half century, as the American public has educated itself about how nature works, a recognition of the value of native ecosystems has become widespread.

This is not a movement confined to fishermen. We aren't even leaders in it. It is a change in how American society perceives the natural world. It is part of the same impulse that gave rise to recycling, the Wilderness Act, the National Environmental Policy Act, the Endangered Species Act, the Clean Air Act, the Clean Water Act, and a long list of other laws and ideas in the past forty years.[24] Conservation experienced a flash point of its own in the 1960s, and anglers and trout are just caught in this bigger movement.

There are some shocks here for fishermen. After a century or so of pretty much having our way with fisheries management agencies (that existed solely to serve us and were largely funded by our license fees), we are annoyed to discover that other people want in, and they have different ideas about the best way to treat fish and the landscapes they inhabit. Many of these people see us—and several generations of fisheries professionals who have done our bidding—as major villains in the creation of Quammen's vale of biological impoverishment, because for most of the time we were in charge of the aquatic scene, all we really wanted was lots of fish to catch, and natives be damned. Ethically, there was no distance between us and those dotty British guys daydreaming about a nice trout stream in some New Zealand meadow.

In the mid-1800s, good fishing was simply defined as catching a huge number of fish of all sizes and probably killing all of them. American colonists and their descendants, released from the laws of Europe, which simply excluded most people except the royal and rich from any right to wildlife, were always very generous with themselves when it came to nature's bounty. But gradually we learned moderation and restraint. For example, we became more aware of the worth of releasing the little ones, not for their own sake, but so that we could catch them again when they were bigger. From that we moved into more rarified realms, wanting to catch them in certain ways—dry flies, nymphs, whatever passion grabbed each of us.

Once we were moving in that direction it was probably inevitable that we would want our quarry to meet more exacting standards as well. By the mid-1900s, hatchery fish began to fall out of favor. We wanted the challenge of "wild" fish, those with the kind of savvy only earned through a life spent in the stream. As mentioned in chapter 2, we wanted to make sure our prey species were worthy of our attention. By this time, releasing fish back into the stream became more important for a new reason. It was seen as a way to further respect the wild environment that sustained them. Most recently, it wasn't all that big a step from preferring wild fish to preferring wild *native* fish, which are now seen by many as providing a more authentic angling experience in wild nature. A fish that actually evolved over many millennia in the water has certain aesthetic advantages over a fish that only arrived a few decades ago.

At each stage in this process of change, a significant number of us stayed behind, content with the old order. Nobody can prove that their view is somehow "right" in any absolute sense. These are subjective and sometimes nearly religious positions. They have to do with deep beliefs about the human relationship with other life forms and with equally heartfelt convictions about the right way to manage natural resources. We will never agree. So it is no surprise that there are now many debates over the restoration or protection of remaining stocks of native fishes.

And let's be clear about the extreme state of things in western waters. This isn't some growing problem, with threats out on the horizon. This has already happened, as comprehensively as it has happened anywhere else on earth. There are amazingly few watersheds left in the Rockies that have anything but token pockets of unaltered fish populations. Every major fly-fishing destination in the Rocky Mountain West is based on a mixture of native and non-native fish, and most of the time the non-native fish are the ones preferred by the anglers. Even such rugged, gruntingly earned mountain country as is protected in Glacier National Park, with all its high tarns and isolated little headwater streams, is down to its last unmanipulated lake; out of all those lovely, remote little bodies of water in that lake-rich hiker's paradise, there is only one

Fish stocking has been so widespread in the West that even the remotest wilderness waters are almost certain to host non-native fish species. Even the rugged high country of Glacier National Park has only one remaining body of water still inhabited solely by native fishes. The St. Mary River, shown here being fished by the late Joe Brooks, isn't it.

Bill Browning, photographer, Montana Historical Society
Photograph Archives, Helena

left with an intact native assemblage of fish unpolluted or uncompromised by non-natives.[25] No wonder people who care about the survival of the West's native species are alarmed.

But much of the heat in today's debates is not focused on the relative qualities or values of native and non-native fish, much less on any moral obligations we might have toward them. Mixed in with disagreements over whether or not native fish are worth saving in principle are other issues. In a celebrated case in Nevada, U.S. Forest Service attempts to protect a population of threatened bull trout have resulted in outright local rebellion against federal laws. Here I think the issue is more the federal laws than the bull trout. Westerners, especially rural westerners, are notoriously unwilling to accept that public lands belong to all Americans and that federal agencies, however clumsy or schizophrenic, are merely trying to exercise some broader public will (add state's rights fanaticism and Sagebrush rebels to the mix).

Attempts to restore westslope cutthroats in Montana are objected to as the wrong way to spend limited fisheries budgets, and the controversy over one of the most ambitious of such projects, on U.S. Forest Service land as well as on Ted Turner's ranch near Bozeman, reeks heavily of local resentment of a rich "outsider." (Add some odd new post-Marxist class struggle to the mix and admit that money is central in every restoration debate.) I always wonder: how much more is Ted Turner an outsider than all the whites who have only preceded him here by a generation, or two generations, or even four or five generations, when other human communities have been here for many thousands of years, and cutthroat trout a lot longer than that. In that long-term scale of things, the difference between Turner and the fourth-generation rancher is statistically, and practically, trivial.

Of course this isn't just a western controversy. For example, Pennsylvania anglers, philosophical descendants of Charles Lose, object to their fish commission's continued devotion to hatchery-bred non-natives. Yet it was the late Ralph Abele, a Pennsylvania agency director, who insisted that American shad be restored to the Susquehanna simply "because they belong there" (add the gunnysack avarice that fish-stocking usually engenders among the public, then pause for a moment of genuine sympathy for the bureaucrats who are, after all, servants of that public and who know that they only get one chance right at the very end of their careers to fall on their swords for what some minority of their constituents regard as a higher cause).[26]

WHAT DO WE REALLY WANT?

There is a swirl of issues here, borne along on a flood of conflicting priorities and passions. But what still intrigues me most is how we came to care so much about natives in the first place. Those of us who feel strongly that native species must be saved spout our inventory of catastrophes—Michigan grayling, Rio Grande cutthroat, silver trout, greenback trout, on and on in emotional overdrive—as if the list alone is proof that something must be done.

But many people hear the list with a kind of "why-don't-you-people-get-a-life?" impatience. We assume too much about the clarity of our purpose. We assume, like all good zealots, that the justness of our cause is obvious when it's not.

The question that is unclear to many people is, Why is nativeness so important? Why should we care? Who's to judge if a native species is in some way "better" than a non-native species? Where do we get off making such judgments on behalf of everybody? After all, some pretty unsavory people have displayed the vilest imaginable bigotry against non-natives of one sort or another (including humans) in the past century or so; are we sure we're on the solid ground we think we are?[27]

Opponents of attempts to save native fish species find it easy to argue that such attempts are quixotic—that we're just a bunch of starry-eyed primitivists who are working our way up to restoring mastodons. Unpersuaded by our aesthetic preferences and moral stance, they argue, naively and incorrectly, that species doesn't matter—that the replacement fish provide roughly the same biomass as the natives and thus fulfill the same ecological role.

More darkly, these opponents wonder if our setting aside the top ends of a few little stream systems for native species is just a foot in the door—if we aren't secretly waiting for the technology to come along that will allow us to conduct a massive "cleansing" of non-native species down the whole length of their favorite river.

They are probably right to wonder about that. I suspect that there are angler-restorationists out there who harbor just such heady, futuristic dreams—the Madison with only cutthroats, grayling, and whitefish, or the Letort and Beaverkill with only brook trout. I have days when those dreams sound pretty good to me, too, so I understand why they would make many anglers nervous.

More important, I assume that eventually some of the non-anglers who have taken such a strong interest in native fish restoration will not just harbor, but openly espouse such startling dreams. If I were a non-angler—just a regular, passionate nature lover—who had sense enough to recognize the exquisite beauty of a wild native trout, and enough wisdom (as I judge wisdom, anyway) to appreciate the even more fundamental beauty of a wild native ecosystem, it's a sure thing I'd be looking to the day when biochemistry gave me the tools to go to the Bighorn River and make it so. Fishermen may not like it, but a lot of very different people love our rivers as much as we do.

But let's set those dreams aside and stick to what we know now. For the forseeable future, the native-trout restorationists' goals seem modest and reasonable, and they have a pretty formidable list of reasons why it's worth the trouble.

The list may as well start with the lofty yet practical admonition of Aldo Leopold, the father of game management in this country, who said that the first rule of intelligent tinkering is to save all the parts.[28] His point was that we don't understand nature well enough to casually cast aside anything it gave us.

A corollary of this rule is that if we lose sight of what we originally had, we have no way of knowing where we're headed. Our little sanctuaries of native species are essentially "trout refuges" that provide baselines against which to measure our treatment of the rest of the aquatic world. Saving native fish and their habitats is in this way a hedge against a future we can't predict and certainly don't understand.

The history of natural-resource management in this country has been a chronicle of discovered purposes—of economic, aesthetic, and social add-ons that have heightened the value of the resources beyond the vision of our ancestors who originated the management system with very little idea where it would have to go, or what it would have to learn, in order to get its job done. It's about time we institutionalize the

*A poignant photograph of the West's past and future
shows an early-twentieth-century catch of native grayling,
but also includes the harbinger of their decline: a single
large rainbow trout, one of the species that replaced
the grayling. The initials on the fly reel suggest that this
catch was made by F. Jay Haynes, the photographer.*

Haynes Foundation Collection, Montana Historical Society
Photograph Archives, Helena

admission of our shortsightedness. As Bruce Farling, executive director of the Montana Council of Trout Unlimited, has
put it, "We should preserve native species for reasons we have
yet to contemplate."[29]

I personally respond to the good sense of this statement
because it perfectly fits with another great experiment in natural-resource management that we have been inadvertently
conducting in the West even longer than we have been messing

with trout populations: Yellowstone Park. Many of the things for which we most cherish Yellowstone now were either barely perceived or not even imagined by the park's founders in 1872. But if the park hadn't been there, and if we hadn't kept ourselves from mucking around with its ecological integrity any more than we have (which was too much anyway), we never would have had the time to think and learn— the time to recognize all the hidden values and treasures that were just waiting there for us to grow up enough to appreciate them.[30] I assume it's the same way with native trout.

This sentiment helps to motivate the conservation community's efforts to protect native aquatic species. For those who can't imagine what harm the loss of some or even many mussel and crayfish species, much less frogs and fish, might do in the long haul, the argument of native-species-as-barometers-of-environmental-health seems a little thin, but the problem is that they *can't* imagine it. The failure is not in the argument. It is in their lack of imagination.

But I suspect that the heart of the argument for native species preservation is more subjective. It lies in matters of morality and responsibility—in an almost inexpressible certainty that we owe it not just to ourselves, but to the whole biosphere not to let anything get away.

It is also to be found in a deepening respect for all these fellow creatures, and the subtle wonder they bring to life. It has been a long time since "What good is it?" was regarded by most rational people as the only necessary question to ask about any species. Why should an animal's fate have to depend upon whether we can make money from it, or get it to grow into a suitable trophy, or catch it on a dry fly? Songbirds bring great joy to our world, but they don't generate a lot of income for most of us; we protect them not to prop up the bird-feeder industry, but because songbirds are really important to us for less pragmatic reasons. We have admitted, in their case, that they are good for us in intangible ways.[31]

Which moves us into the misty realms of the human spirit, where I suspect most of us put our strongest emphasis when we campaign for native trout—Yeah, yeah, there's all that practical stuff, but this is fishing we're talking about here, and we love it for where it takes us and what we find there. Trout Unlimited President Charles Gauvin describes the powerful intangibles of wild native trout in terms of authenticity and tradition:

> The willingness to seek out native coldwater fish in their historical habitats—and to recreate those habitats where feasible—should be a quality that distinguishes trout and salmon anglers. . . . When you hike into the high country of the West in pursuit of native trout, you bask in the ethereal splendor of the landscape that caught the eye of Thomas Moran. While there, you expect to see elk and, if you're lucky, a bighorn sheep or a grizzly; you don't expect to see Siberian tigers. As anglers, we should have the same sensibility about fish; we should place a special value on waters that are free of non-natives because those waters are ingredients of the landscape as Moran found it. The same applies to fishing for

brookies in their native range. I love to catch rainbows, but not in Thoreau's Maine Woods, thank
you.[32]

Last, there is this. Protection and restoration of wild,
native ecoystems, for all the practical obstacles and political
heat, are robust new missions of our society. This change is
not going to go away. It is driven by people who believe that
humans have no right to let native species go extinct, or to
casually displace them, or reduce them to tiny fragments of
what they once were. Many of these people do not fish.
Most of them probably do not feel strongly one way or
another about fishing, but that is changing too, and not in
our favor.

We anglers have grown complacent. We think of ourselves
as thoughtful, concerned conservationists. But the world is
not impressed.

CHOICES, ESPECIALLY MINE

Anglers have a choice here. We can fight the change, and
no doubt we can win a lot of battles. At least we can gum up
the works for a while.

Or, we can put the same energy into understanding what
is behind the changes and figuring out what is in it for us,
both practically and spiritually. Enlightened self-interest is
still hard to beat as a bargaining position.

Based on my own experiences with native trout and the
ecosystems they inhabit, and on what I have learned from all
the conservation biologists, ecosystem managers, sportsmen,

nature-lovers, and restoration ecologists who are struggling to save native species, I have decided that there are many good reasons to save and restore these fish. If called upon, I can trot these reasons out and wave them around just to prove how carefully I've thought this through. But "because they belong there" is all the reason I really need.

*Happy fly fisher Frances Jurgens Kleinschmidt Tobie
proudly displayed her catch, circa the 1920s.*

CHAPTER EIGHT

Fly Fishing as If It Matters

It is useless to argue the question as to whether,
or no, fly-fishing is worthy of serious thought.
A definite conclusion can never be arrived at
because so much can be said for and against.

—J. C. Mottram, *Fly Fishing:*
Some New Arts and Mysteries (1915)

About thirty years ago, the first time I float-fished in Montana, my guide was all but archetypical—a beaming face seamed and weathered by hundreds of days astream in the Midwest, Alaska, and the northern Rockies; clothes worn to that perfect state of picturesque disrepair that can be achieved only by long repetitive outdoor activity; and a hint of independence even greater than normal for hardy professional outdoorsmen. He'd occasionally begin a yarn with, "Now back in my poachin' days . . . ."

We drifted easily along in his McKenzie boat. The river had split into multiple channels like a loose braid of small creeks, and we'd left the main current to explore one smaller channel.

The fishing action was about medium, and the day was bright except for a few rain squalls. The small channel was a welcome change from the overpowering presence of the big river. For half a mile, we moved quickly from pool to pool, stopping only for a streamside lunch and a quick snooze in the sun. Then, just as we were wondering when our little channel would rejoin the main stream, our way was blocked by three heavy fence wires strung loosely across the channel. As the boat nosed against them, the guide rummaged through the duffel under his seat and came up with an immense pair of pliers, with which he twisted the wires one by one until they broke. As they sank and we drifted over them, he remarked impatiently, "They ain't supposed to do that. This here's a navigable waterway and can't be blocked."

A little later we discovered that he was wrong, or at least maybe not as right as he had imagined. A low dam, complete with a high wood-rail fence, raised the channel several feet. We spent nearly an hour dismantling a section of fence, wrestling the boat over the dam, and then chasing it downstream after it dropped into the water below. We put the fence back together as well as we could there at the dam, but it didn't occur to us to go back upstream and try to fix the wires.

Rivers, like the fish and wildlife they support, have always presented lawmakers with difficult challenges. Perhaps foremost among these is the matter of defining and regulating the use of a publicly owned natural resource that refuses to sit still. Rivers may be even more troublesome than geese, deer, or raccoons; whereas the latter only eat a person's garden and crap all over the lawn, the former may wash away his land. Rivers tend to meander and shift, taking from one property (or town, county, state, or nation) and adding to another, or taking from both and creating an island in midstream, or simply chewing away at the land until everybody has less. Or, if mobility isn't enough, the river may just disappear for a few months now and then. Rivers are very unreliable boundaries.

More than a century ago, when John Wesley Powell and the other early government surveyors were charting the western wilderness, they became the first to point out that water supplies would be the limiting factor in the development and use of the region. The lesson has been ignored repeatedly since then, but it has not changed.

For better or worse, since those early and sometimes violent contests over water rights, a sprawling, inexact legal code has developed—just as it did in the rest of the country—to regulate the use of this always-too-limited resource. In the modern West, the big battles over water (concerning impoundments, slurry lines, coal-plant withdrawals, irrigation, and the like) are fought through the mechanisms of this elaborate legal code.[1] The existence of the code—a tangle of sometimes conflicting federal, state, and county statutes—is why the impatience of my guide that day is worth remembering at all.

My guide's behavior and attitudes seem to me to be powerfully illustrative of fly fishing's value as "a way in" to the greater western narrative of which it has long been a neglected thread. When he pulled those huge pliers from under his seat, he activated our very own little chapter in some of western history's most colorful sagas—the anguish of too little of a given resource with too many users, the debates over public and private property rights, the "class struggles" of traditional extractive users versus recreational users, and (this was especially appropriate so close to Virginia City) a satisfying episode of authentic vigilantism.

Fly fishing intersects the greater western story in so many ways that it surprises me that more writers—besides historians—have not sensed its rhetorical and scholarly opportunities. As fly fishing's practitioners grow in economic power, political reach, ecological awareness, and clarity of need, those intersections will only become more compelling.

I realize that writers on the West have plenty to do and that we aren't necessarily doing as good a job as the West deserves even with the topics we favor, but I also wonder about our selectivity. The historians among us, having in recent decades called into question all the grand, stereotypical old Wild West images, still show strong fidelity to certain topics. We may have abandoned (or at least tastefully moderated) the glorification of the Euramerican conquest of the West, but a lot of us still dote on its violence.

Consider the Battle of the Little Bighorn. As important as that battle directly and indirectly was in western history, and as important as it deservedly became to both native and Euramerican cultures, let's face it: a lot of the modern interest in it doesn't seem to have as much to do with politics and culture as with (to borrow from Ellis Peters) a "morbid taste for bones"—our apparently insatiable fascination with the gory details.

That we find so much glory in those bones is not unusual; if you want to see historic-battlefield glory in its full industrial flower, spend a couple hours driving through the "marble orchards" of Gettsyburg. I also know that once historians take hold of a divisive and tremendously symbolic subject like this, they never let go, and never stop reconsidering what earlier historians said. It's just what we do. Such scenes of raw human violence become places of great, enduring power. I feel it when I go there, every time. After all the years since my first visit to the battlefield, I still cannot return to or even think of the Little Bighorn without yet again enjoying the justice I find in the outcome of that battle.

But at the same time, battlefields always make me wonder about the historical profession's—and the public's—sense of proportion. Maybe they make the complexities and conflicts of human existence a little too easy, bringing it all down to the day of complete failure when there's nothing left to do but start killing each other. Maybe they aren't the history so much as its aftereffects.

I wouldn't for a moment suggest that the story of western fly fishing measures up in significance to the story of how native and non-native westerners so persistently and successfully slaughtered each other. But when it comes to details, let's keep our eyes and minds open. As historian Ken Owens has pointed out, while Custer and his soldiers were being wiped out on the Little Bighorn, General George Crook and his men were one drainage over indulging in a great trout-fishing binge that went on for several days and seems to have been, for at least some of the men, one of the most memorable experiences of the entire war.[2]

In a traditional historian's telling of this situation, Crook and his men would have been "doing nothing" or "wasting

*Outdoor writers John Gartner's and Claude Kreider's
faces reflect their good luck fishing Montana's Swan River,
probably in the 1960s.*

Bill Browning, photographer, Montana Historical Society
Photograph Archives, Helena

time fishing" while Custer died. In fact and instead, they
were doing something that was both unforgettable and cul-
turally significant.

So at the risk of beating a dead trout, I'll consider Mottram's
unanswerable question from the epigraph, and wonder about
a few more unanswered questions of western fishing history.[3]
In my introduction and elsewhere in this book, I've already
proposed both justifications and avenues for such study, and
referred to the suggestions of other writers. Fly fishing

already matters to many westerners. It stands a fair chance of mattering to whatever professional thinkers care to give it a shot.

Custer and Crook bring an obvious opportunity to mind. Surely, the preponderance of active, even passionate, sportsmen among the military leadership in the West of this period is neither an accident nor a mere matter of historical trivia. Wherever I have looked in my own studies of the West, I have been struck by the intense and widespread interest of career military men not only in hunting and fishing, but also in conservation.[4] How did that happen, and why did it work?[5]

The growing literature on the history and culture of American hunting provides some wonderful models for studies that should be applied to angling, and the West provides fertile fields for such application. Stuart Marks's *Southern Hunting in Black and White: Nature, History, and Ritual in a Carolina Community* (1991) seems eminently adaptable as a form of inquiry about western angling history. Marks's study of racial, class, gender, economic, and ecological issues associated with a tri-racial human hunting community reminded me on almost every page of how exciting and illuminating it would be to have a similar portrayal of the fishing community in my home county here in Montana, or in many other counties where fly fishing is similarly valued.

My popularly written *American Fly Fishing: A History* (1987), though it undeniably tells the reader a lot of important stuff about the subject, is barely a beginning in regard to the kinds of inquiries awaiting us—it may serve best by exposing interesting situations and questions that need more attention. The model provided by Daniel Herman's *Hunting and the American Imagination* (2001), a study of the dramatic changes in how society has perceived hunting and hunters, seems perfectly applicable to western angling. The way society views fishing and fishermen in the West has been anything but static.

In opportunities like these, I am especially excited by the possibilities for placing fly fishing in the greater context of the whole community of anglers. I've often referred to fly fishing as a "sub-culture" in the larger culture of angling; this may have been a shaky informalism in terminology on my part, but I think it has served to make the points that we fly fishers are, on the one hand, like a lot of other people who want to catch fish, and, on the other hand, pretty different from them too—especially in our own minds. Where has that come from, and where has it led?

J. C. Mottram's unanswerable question, about the possible worth of thinking seriously about fly fishing, gets answered all the time. If it wasn't worth thought, it couldn't support the continuing flood of new fly-fishing books, the electronic morass of fly-fishing websites, and the last thirty years' incredible proliferation of magazines that are devoted exclusively or largely to this one sport.[6] Volume output alone does not prove that much or any of this thinking is deep, smart, or even helpful, but it's certainly proof of a vibrant, energetic bunch of people who seem to have a lot on their minds.

Those of us who believe that thought is a good thing often get to feeling like we're a minority these days. It would be a nice, affirmative gesture toward the anglers among us, and a

lot of fun besides, if some hospitable institute, library, or university were to sponsor a workshop-style symoposium with
the sole purpose of producing a tentative research agenda for
western fly fishing, one broad enough to include fisheries
management and ecological studies as well as history, sociol-
ogy, economics, and literature.

We who fly fish seem to think about it all the time. We may
not think hard enough, or historically enough, or broadly
enough, or critically enough, but there's no doubt in our
minds that our thoughts are serious. That they're also fun
just makes the fishing better.

Acknowledgments

Traditionally in the acknowledgments section of a book, the spouse is listed last, but then described in glowing terms as the real force behind the author's work. If someone is that all-fired important, they ought to be listed right off, so here's to my wife and hero Marsha Karle, who makes it all possible.

John Varley, my friend and frequent co-author in a number of formal and informal publications about trout and conservation, has been one of North America's most effective champions of intelligent management of wild trout ecosystems. He has often been the greatest influence on my thinking in these realms. Bud Lilly, guide, conservationist, co-author, and fishing pal, has on occasions beyond counting provided the perspective of the historical witness to western fly fishing and its rich, quirky ways. Robert Behnke, through his grand books and a long correspondence, has also helped with many historical matters.

Though many editors and others, listed below, read portions of the manuscript, I'm especially grateful to Ken Owens and Adrian Bantjes who reviewed the manuscript for the Montana Historical Society Press and made many smart suggestions for its improvement.

The folks at the Montana Historical Society Press, including Clint Attebery, Glenda Bradshaw, Molly Holz, Tammy Ryan, and Clark Whitehorn, have been very good to this book project, as have the staff of the Montana Historical Society Research Center who provided able assistance in the Library and Photograph Archives. I am a longtime and enthusiastic member of the Montana Historical Society, so it's a special treat for me to have books published by them. It's also fun to work with a publisher that has a world-class collection of western photographs right down the hall. Thanks also to Mike Korn for his saddled trout illustration and for drawing the flies that close each chapter.

Rick Balkin, my literary agent and friend for some twenty years now, provided his customary sage advice and guidance.

Though I've tried to keep the narrative conversational, I've also tried to provide adequate formal citations, which also serve as precise acknowledgments of the many other biologists, managers, historians, storytellers, and other writers who have led me to such wonderful lore, data, rumors, ideas, stories, episodes, and adventures in western fly fishing.

More than most of my earlier books, this one has gone through a complicated gestation as essays and stories. All the previously published material in this book has been worked over, sometimes beyond recognition, until it seemed a part of the greater enterprise of the book. But as I look over the chapters I can still identify the following chunks and larger pieces, and I thank the editors of these publications for their interest and editorial insights.

The introduction is partly based on material first published in *Trout* and *Montana The Magazine of Western History.* It also contains some material first presented on June 9, 2000, at the opening ceremony of the Museum of the Rockies's splendid fly-fishing exhibit, *The Lore and Lure of Western Fly Fishing*, Bozeman, Montana. My thanks to the staff of that wonderful institution for inviting me to be guest curator of the exhibit, and then for doing all the work.

Chapter 1 is mostly from *Big Sky Journal,* though the Rudyard Kipling material is based in good part on an article I published long ago in *The American Fly Fisher.* It was, in fact, a toss-up whether I would include a revised version of that article in this book rather than the chapter about Edward Hewitt that I did include. I finally chose Hewitt because he was more interesting as an angling authority and his writings gave me more room to explore some interesting ideas than did Kipling's better written and perhaps more superficially entertaining account.

Chapter 2 is from *Montana The Magazine of Western History.* Former editor Clark Whitehorn's enthusiasm for fly-fishing history has probably had as much to do with me deciding to prepare this book as anything else.

Chapter 3 appeared in *The American Fly Fisher.* This is the quarterly journal of the American Museum of Fly Fishing, and until recent years stood alone as a regular publisher of research on fly-fishing history.

Chapter 4 appeared in *Annals of Wyoming.* I am grateful to Adrian Bantjes of the University of Wyoming for involving me in the special fly-fishing-related issue of this fine publication. Richard Hoffmann, York University, provided a very helpful critical reading of an earlier draft of this chapter and suggested several excellent interpretive avenues. Yellowstone National Park Historian Lee Whittlesey read the manuscript and offered several good suggestions. The work on this chapter parallels far more extensive work I have been involved in, supported by the National Park Service, on the history of wildlife in greater Yellowstone—a project that Lee Whittlesey and I have shared productively for more than ten years. I am pleased, at least in this one small instance, to bring attention to Yellowstone's historic trout the way we have brought attention to its historic charismatic megafauna in many other publications.

Portions of chapter 5 appeared in *American Angler* and *Fly Fishing News, Views, and Reviews*. Richard Hoffmann provided a "translation" of the original pseudo-Latin description of the salmonfly and otherwise helped with historical matters. The staffs of the Montana State University Libraries, the Linnean Society of London, Yellowstone National Park Research Library, and the London Horticultural Society were all of great help. As in so many western fishing matters, Bud Lilly has been helpful with valuable historical and technical insights, about his and others' use of salmonflies; his own experience dates back to the 1920s. My acquaintance with George Grant, which involved a good deal of communication in the 1970s and 1980s, has also been a special treat.

Chapter 6 was first presented as a keynote address to the annual Friends of the Montana State University Libraries Banquet, Montana State University, October 11, 2001. It was revised and presented to a University of Wyoming History

Department seminar, spring 2002.

Portions of chapter 7 had previous lives in *The American Fly Fisher, American Angler,* and *Fly Rod and Reel.* Robert Behnke, emeritus professor at Colorado State University, has been a special help and inspiration in understanding the human redistribution of trout in North America.

Some passages in chapter 8 first appeared in *Fly Rod and Reel.*

Notes

1. Thomas Barker, *Barker's Delight, or the Art of Angling* (London: Humphrey Moseley, 1659), 34.

2. I have written about this process of changing values in angling in previous publications. See, especially, the essay "Trout Family Values," in *Royal Coachman: The Lore and Legends of Fly Fishing* (New York: Simon and Schuster, 1999), 186–200; and two extended passages in *Real Alaska: Finding Our Way in the Wild Country* (Mechanicsburg, Pa.: Stackpole Books, 2001), 154–61, 180–201.

3. Schullery, *Royal Coachman*, 17. I don't mean to suggest that fly fishing was never fashionable. It has long been fashionable in the sense that many fly fishers regarded themselves as the most stylish or tasteful of all people who fished. I discuss this point on several occasions in *American Fly Fishing: A History* (New York: Lyons Press, 1987). However, to an extent never before imagined or expected by fly fishers, starting in the 1970s, fly fishing became fashionable among that portion of American society who, regardless of their previous interest or disinterest in the outdoors, were generally known as the most fashionable.

4. I served as guest curator of this regional exhibit. I don't feel bashful about praising it because my title was largely honorary, and other people, under the leadership of museum

curator Beth Merrick, did all the real work.

5. *Montana The Magazine of Western History* 52, no. 2 (Summer 2002).

6. *Annals of Wyoming* 76, no. 2 (Spring 2004).

7. I do not mean to suggest that fly fishing has received no academic attention. There has been some, for quite a while, and I will cite it now and then as it applies to the essays in this book.

For now, let me call attention to just one book that proposes to do just the kinds of things I'm talking about here: William Washabaugh and Catherine Washabaugh's *Deep Trout: Angling in Popular Culture* (New York: Berg, 2000). This book serves well as an example of the risks fly fishing will face as it climbs into the academic light. The senior author is an anthropologist. The book is a quick swing through fly fishing's literature and society. The authors dip selectively into fishing literature, visit some of fly fishing's historic sites, take some shots at modern trout conservation, and, in general, apply a magnificent condescension to the whole enterprise of fly fishing, finding most of it wanting in one way or another (though they do seem to admire some fly fishers, and the senior author is said to be a fly fisher). Fly fishers are, evidently, even more self-serving and misguided than the most cynical among us imagined. Or maybe not. At least, maybe this book doesn't really prove it. The historical and background research in the book, at least as that research involves angling, is typically superficial and sometimes embarrassingly inaccurate, giving the impression of an undergraduate paper in which the writer has shopped through the handy source material for accommodating quotations but has not taken on the far harder challenge of grasping any part of the topic's richness.

In any case, I guess we have to start somewhere, and maybe this book will be one of those starts. At least it would give other students some issues to argue about. Buried among the book's snap judgments and posturings are many good ideas and historical points that have been gathered from the academic literature and applied to fishing, some perhaps even for the first time. As I said, this process of formal examination and criticism isn't going to be easy.

A more concise and helpful discussion of some of the same issues surrounding modern fly fishing appears in Adrian Franklin, *Animals & Modern Cultures* (Sage Publications: London, 1999), especially chapter 6, "Naturalizing Sports: Hunting and Angling in Modernity," 105–25. Franklin, a Tasmanian sociologist, sets the historical stage well, if briefly, and offers many comparisons between the respective hunting and angling societies of the U.K., U.S., and Australia.

8. More than twenty years ago, when the Federation of Fly Fishers was in the process of making West Yellowstone their headquarters, FFF vice president Martin Seldon told me that the organization thought of Yellowstone Park as their "philosophical home" because park managers had pioneered so many important changes in sport-fishing regulations. This, as much as the park's famous fishing itself, has continued to give Yellowstone a leading role (or "privileged" role, as I have seen it described) in the modern fly-fishing community.

A subject I do not explore in this book but that is already showing interesting developments in the West is the multiplicity of "homes" and "centers" and even points of origin for western fly fishing. As I have suggested in other writings, the East is blessed and cursed with a number of competing "cradles" and "birthplaces" of fly fishing, including Long Island, Massachusetts, the Catskills, the Poconos, and the Cumberland Valley, all of which sustain claims of being the most important point of origin for American fly fishing. Already here in the West, similar regional claims are appearing—for Jackson Hole, or Colorado, or Montana, or

Wyoming, or some other spot. I suppose that I had hoped, naively I now see, that we wouldn't have to go through that out here. None of the cases made are convincing, too often being based not on actual historical documentation, but on commercial ambitions or simple self-centeredness instead. The idea that a sport could be simultaneously fostered and developed in many places at once seems less attractive to local interests than the self-flattery of being at the center of the universe, even such a modest universe as fly fishing.

CHAPTER I

"YE GODS! THAT WAS FISHING"

1. Rudyard Kipling, *American Notes* (New York: Arcadia House, 1950), 119.

2. Ibid., 119.

3. For more on Yankee Jim and his toll road, see Aubrey Haines, *The Yellowstone Story,* 2 vols. (Boulder: Colorado Associated University Press, 1977), 2:1; and Jack E. Haynes, "That Man, Yankee Jim," *Rotospoke* 4 (December 28, 1954): 2–3.

4. Kipling, *American Notes,* 120–21.

5. Andrew Herd, *The Fly* (Ellesmere, U.K.: Medlar Press, 2001), especially chapter 5, which is an excellent summary of the state of tackle in Kipling's time. It should be supplemented, for the social side of the story, with Ken Cameron's essay, "The Victorian Angler," *American Fly Fisher* 7 (Winter 1980): 2–7.

6. Washabaugh and Washabaugh in *Deep Trout* state that fly-fishing techniques "imported into the United States from England" were "dramatically altered to match the social conditions of their new cultural bed" (p. 18). Actually, the mechanics of fly-fishing techniques, such as casting, presentation of the fly, landing the fish, and so on, changed only

modestly for many years. Much else, including what I have elsewhere called the angler's "cultural baggage" did change, even dramatically, and the West is a great place to study that change. Examples of how fly fishing changed in the West consume much of the present book. But Washabaugh and Washabaugh are incorrect when they suggest that the American fly fisher somehow abruptly revolutionized the millennia-old practices by which the angler delivered the fly to the water and retrieved the hooked fish from the water. There is no evidence for this. Fly-fishing techniques continued to develop and experience refinement and change and, indeed, did so at a faster pace after 1800 than they had before.

7. Craig Mathews and John Juracek, *Fly Patterns of Yellowstone* (West Yellowstone, Mont.: Blue Ribbon Flies, 1987), 42. The concepts of beauty and ugliness in fly patterns are largely unconsidered; the whole matter of the aesthetics of this craft (or, as some have described it, folk art) deserves considerably more attention than it has received.

8. Sylvester Nemes, *The Soft-Hackled Fly* (Old Greenwich, Conn: Chatham Press, 1975); Sylvester Nemes, *The Soft-Hackled Fly Addict* (Chicago: privately printed, 1981); Sylvester Nemes, *Soft-Hackled Fly Imitations* (Bozeman, Mont.: privately printed, 1991).

9. Paul Schullery, "Aelian Lives," *American Angler* 26 (January/February 2003): 20–25, is a summary of current thinking on the origins of this long tradition of simple wet flies.

10. Mock deification, some of it seeming nearly the real thing, has characterized much of the worshipfulness angling writers, at least, have aimed at their great figures. There is a sizeable literature on spirituality as an aspect of nature appreciation, and though the nature-church idea is quite old, the modern environmental movement has often been criticized or just noted for its spiritual overtones. Joel Daehnke's *In the Work of the Their Hands Is Their Prayer: Cultural*

Narrative and Redemption on the American Frontiers, 1830–1930 (Athens: Ohio University Press, 2003), 197–202, has an interesting discussion of one perennial topic involving angling and religion, the appropriateness of fishing on the Sabbath.

11. Kipling, *American Notes,* 123.

CHAPTER 2
FLY FISHING IN WESTERN CULTURE

1. For a helpful and insightful discussion of the same questions I consider in this chapter, see Adrian Bantjes, "Nature, Culture, and the Fly-Fishing History of Wyoming and the Rocky Mountain West," *Annals of Wyoming* 76, no. 2 (Spring 2004): 41–53. I consider Bantjes's essay; Ken Owens's "Fishing the Hatch: New West Romanticism and Fly-fishing the High Country," *Montana The Magazine of Western History* 52, no. 2 (Summer 2002): 10–19; and the present chapter to be the three best attempts to provide something approaching a framework for the direction of future scholarly inquiries into fly fishing's history and culture.

2. For a recent account of the rise of skiing as a key element of western "culture," see Annie Gilbert Coleman, *Ski Style, Sport and Culture in the Rockies* (Lawrence: University Press of Kansas, 2004).

3. The works of Walter Prescott Webb and Bernard DeVoto seem to be the most often cited sources on the West as colony, but see "Denial and Dependence," at the beginning of chapter 3 of Patricia Nelson Limerick's *The Legacy of Conquest: The Unbroken Past of the American West* (New York: W. W. Norton, 1987), 78–87, for a nice discussion of the ways in which westerners have, for more than a century, unhappily perceived themselves as territories, colonies, or otherwise subsidiaries of the East.

4. Patricia Nelson Limerick, *Something in the Soil: Legacies and Reckonings in the New West* (New York: W. W. Norton, 2000), 102.

5. Ken Cameron, "Real West," *Waterlog* 22 (June/July 2000): 31.

6. Ibid.

7. Ibid.

8. For a very helpful overview of the rise of modern western fly-fishing commerce, see Owens, "Fishing the Hatch," 10–19.

9. Cameron, "Real West," 31.

10. Ibid.

11. See especially the chapter, "The Imagined West," in Richard White's textbook, *"It's Your Misfortune and None of My Own": A New History of the American West* (Norman: University of Oklahoma Press, 1991), 613–32.

12. Heroism is certainly one of the least explored aspects of angling's intellectual history. Beyond the obvious noting of certain popular character types, such as the anti-heroism of poachers, trout bums, and other inhabitants of the social edges, not much has been made of angling's powerful enthusiasm for its own celebrities. It would be a rewarding exercise for someone to start with, say, Joseph Campbell's *The Hero with a Thousand Faces* (Princeton, N.J.: Princeton University Press, 1968); and Kent Steckmesser's *The Western Hero in History and Legend* (Norman: University of Oklahoma Press, 1965) and then read a whole lot of western angling writing in their light and let us know what they make of it.

13. Hal Rothman, "Shedding Skin and Shifting Shape: Tourism in the Modern West," in *Seeing and Being Seen: Tourism in the American West,* ed. David M. Wrobel and Patrick T. Long (Lawrence: University of Kansas Press and the Center of the American West, 2001), 101. A curious thing

about visiting fly fishers in the West is that it is extremely likely that most of them don't even think of themselves as tourists. Or, if they do, they see themselves as a highly rarified form of the species, not subject to the routine stereotypes and ridicule given the common tourist.

14. See, for example, Charles Brooks, *The Trout and the Stream* (New York: Crown, 1974); and Charles Brooks, *Nymph Fishing for Larger Trout* (New York: Crown, 1976), which between them cover the theoretical ground plowed by Charles Brooks.

15. Anglers who are inclined to regard their longer local residence as a reason to look down on more recent arrivals should read David Wrobel's discussion of the urge of westerners to judge each other in terms of their relative "westernness"—a competitive measure of their personal authenticity in place—in the chapter section titled "Primacy, Authenticity, Promise, and Place," in David M. Wrobel, *Promised Lands: Promotion, Memory, and the Creation of the American West* (Lawrence: University of Kansas Press, 2002), 185–89.

16. I am not originating anything in this suggestion that the landscape's power brings on mythic sentiments about adventure and heroism. Generations of travel writers, nature writers, and scholars have commented on these same notions. I am, however, offering them as striking examples of how fly fishing in the West fits beautifully into the greater context of regional history.

CHAPTER 3

YELLOWSTONE I

1. Daniel Defoe, *Robinson Crusoe* (New York: Dodd Mead, 1940), 79.

2. John McDonald, *The Origins of Angling* (New York: Lyons and Burford, 1997), 3. My thanks especially to Richard

Hoffmann, York University, Toronto, for conversations on definitions and the intellectual history of sport.

3. David Sansone, *Greek Athletics and the Genesis of Sport* (Berkeley: University of California Press, 1988), 31. Sansone, incidentally, also serves as a type specimen of a scholar who can switch from a serious discussion of the history of competitive games to poorly thought-out moralizing and casual theorizing about the blood sports; see pages 31–32 of his book for a classic example of trivializing hunting and fishing in order to dismiss them.

4. There are, for example, still those of us whose love for baseball became muted in the early 1960s, when what we saw as an essential institutional constant of the sport—two major leagues with a total of sixteen teams—was discarded. I still love to watch baseball being played because of its inherent beauty as a game, but I have almost completely lost interest in its formerly satisfying statistical memory, which, for me at least, was too gravely compromised by league expansion to matter any more.

5. Adrian A. Bantjes, "Introduction: Bourdieu on the Bighorn? Or, Towards a Cultural History of Fly-Fishing in Wyoming and the American West," *Annals of Wyoming* 76, no. 2 (Spring 2004): 3.

For those unfamiliar with fishing writing, I should emphasize that the lack of scholarly attention to fishing history has not been mirrored by a lack of non-academic writing about fishing history. Countless popularly written fishing books contain historical material, much of it available nowhere else. Like countless local historians and small historical societies, the writers of these books are performing a valuable service by saving so much information that would otherwise be vulnerable to loss.

This historical writing has taken many forms. There are some wonderful compilations of historically significant fly patterns, for example. A surprising number of notable anglers have been the subject of popularly written biographies. One of the most important and sizeable subsets of popularly written angling history is the club history—that is, the story of a specific fishing club—of which there are hundreds.

For an excellent sampler of the variety and volume of this work, see Henry T. Bruns, *Angling Books of the Americas* (Atlanta: Angler's Press, 1975), itself an example of the skill of the dedicated amateur historian of angling; it is the most comprehensive bibliography of its type.

And there are a number of popularly written book-length works on the history of fishing, including my own book, *American Fly Fishing*. Some of these are quite fine. Andrew Herd's recent overview history of fly fishing, *The Fly* (Shropshire, U.K.: Medlar Press, 2003), is disciplined, penetrating, and wisely opinionated.

A last thought here. At one point in its long and extremely wordy adventure, fishing literature has poked its head above the crowd, and that is in the pages of Izaak Walton's *Compleat Angler,* a book so masterfully written that many would probably agree is famous despite its subject. Here I admit an exception to the shortage of scholarship relating to the history of angling. Walton's work and life are abundantly studied and served by scholars.

6. Hunting has fared far better than fishing at the hands of modern historical scholars, but considering just the immense numbers of people who have participated in sport hunting in North America in the past five hundred years, it has received an amazingly small amount of scholarly attention. Still, it is far ahead of sport fishing, and I am grateful for the attention it has received. Among the book-length works that have made important progress and provide excellent examples for potential historians of sport fishing, I include Matt Cartmill, *A View to a Death in the Morning:*

Hunting and Nature through History (Cambridge, Mass.: Harvard University Press, 1993); Daniel Justin Herman, *Hunting and the American Imagination* (Washington, D.C.: Smithsonian Institution, 2001); Stuart A. Marks, *Southern Hunting in Black and White: Nature, History, and Ritual in a Carolina Community* (Princeton, N.J.: Princeton University Press, 1991); and John Reiger, *American Sportsmen and the Origins of Conservation*, 3d rev. ed. (Corvallis: Oregon State University Press, 2001). Just a quick cruise through the references in these four books will lead you to many other works of sport-hunting history and topics that border that subject in one way or another.

7. Herman, *Hunting in the American Imagination,* 160. The rise of the hunter-naturalist is a global story of the nineteenth century, which is generally seen as culminating in the United States in the writings of Theodore Roosevelt, who was regarded, with some justification, not only as one of the best hunting writers of his day, but one of the leading "faunal naturalists." See Paul R. Cutright, *Theodore Roosevelt the Naturalist* (New York: Harper and Brothers, 1956); and Paul R. Cutright, *Theodore Roosevelt: The Making of a Conservationist* (Urbana: University of Illinois Press, 1985).

8. Karen Wonders, "A Sportsman's Eden, Part I: A Wilderness Beckons," *The Beaver* 79, no. 5 (October/November, 1999): 28. It is hard to overemphasize the importance of the pioneering overview of the activities of sportsmen, as both naturalists and conservationists, written by Reiger, in *American Sportsmen and the Origins of Conservation.*

9. I can think of few more potentially interesting angling-related studies waiting to be written than "The Angler as Nature Observer: Five Centuries of Literary Inquiry." I am not aware of a scholarly or popular study of natural history as an element of angling literature, but the presence of brief natural history essays was a standard element of many British

angling books in the seventeenth, eighteenth, and nineteenth centuries. The natural history interests of the hunters described by Herman were often confined primarily to information that would help them kill the game. Theodore Roosevelt would complain about this narrowness of interest and exemplified a somewhat broader tradition of hunter-naturalist. The narrower focus was most common among the earlier angling writers as well. Before 1800, Walton's *Compleat Angler,* especially the later editions published during his lifetime, may have been among the most extraordinary in its breadth of natural history authorities cited, and Walton buttressed these citations (some of which, though authoritative for his day, we now know to have been absurdly wrong) with his own observations or those of trusted acquaintances.

10. Thaddeus Norris, *The American Angler's Book* (Philadelphia: Butler, 1864); Genio Scott, *Fishing in American Waters* (New York: Harper, 1869).

11. John Reiger, in *American Sportsmen and the Origins of Conservation,* introduces a number of these figures who led dual professional careers in the late 1800s.

12. I am well aware of the loaded and politically complicated nature of the word "subsistence" today. Because of controversies over the subsistence rights and claims of native people, natural-resource managers in many parts of the world face daunting conflicts among user groups. For the interest groups in these struggles, "subsistence" has taken on a life of provocation, evoking feelings and responses far beyond the dictionary meaning of the word. In North American natural-resource management circles, it would probably be difficult to use the word in a conversation without your listeners reflexively picturing some battle, quarrel, or court case they know about or even participated in. Like "environment" or "national security," "subsistence" has become more a fire-starter than a word.

Still, I have a lot of faith in the durability of good words with clear definitions, so I think it's the right word for me to use in this chapter in its simpler, less socially burdened sense. By "subsistence" I really do mean just the catching of fish to eat them. I'm not applying any of the formal legal meanings or complicated social trappings that have adhered to the word in the course of many well-known controversies, as important as I think those meanings and controversies are. "Subsistence"just seems the best word for my purposes. I considered "survival," but it implies a degree of desperation that I do not intend.

13. The most useful works on the Washburn Party's background include Nathaniel Langford, *The Discovery of Yellowstone Park* (Lincoln: University of Nebraska Press, 1972), especially Aubrey Haines's foreword, vii–xxi; Aubrey Haines, *Yellowstone National Park: Its Exploration and Establishment* (Washington, D.C.: National Park Service, 1974), 54–99, 137–52; and Richard A. Bartlett, *Nature's Yellowstone* (Albuquerque: University of New Mexico Press, 1974), 164–207. For more on Langford particularly, see Paul Schullery and Lee H. Whittlesey, *Myth and History in the Creation of Yellowstone National Park* (Lincoln: University of Nebraska Press, 2003).

14. Johan Huizinga, *Homo Ludens: A Study of the Play-Element in Culture* (Boston: Beacon Press, 1955), i. The book was apparently first published in English translation in 1950, though the passages I quote were dated 1938.

15. General background on the Washburn Party members, as provided in this essay, is from the publications of Langford, Haines, and Bartlett, as cited above. For a helpful discussion of the distinction between exploration and discovery, especially as it applied to the West, see William Goetzmann, *Exploration and Empire: The Explorer and the Scientist in the Winning of the American West* (Austin: Texas State Historical Association, 1993), xi–xv. For a consideration of

how sport anglers of the rising leisure class of this period saw angling as an aspect of "national manhood," see Daehnke, *In the Work of Their Hands Is Their Prayer*, 156–212. Though I would cheerfully quibble with a number of Daehnke's interpretations and specific comments, I am especially pleased to see this extended use made of the angling literature in a scholarly commentary on anything to do with the larger questions of American life. For new interpretations and language by which to understand the early experience of Yellowstone Park, see Gregory Clark, *Rhetorical Landscapes in America: Variations on a Theme from Kenneth Burke* (Columbia: University of South Carolina Press, 2004), especially chapter 4, "Transcendence at Yellowstone."

16. Walter Trumbull, "The Washburn Yellowstone Expedition," *Overland Monthly* 6 (May 1871): 431.

17. Cornelius Hedges, "Excerpts from the Diary of Cornelius Hedges (July 6, 1870 to January 29, 1871), transcribed from the original diary in the Montana Historical Society Research Center by Aubrey Haines, November 5, 1962," manuscript 2, Yellowstone National Park Research Library, Gardiner, Montana.

18. Walter Trumbull, "Yellowstone Papers, No. One," *Rocky Mountain Daily Gazette*, October 18, 1870, 2.

19. Hedges, "Diary," 3.

20. Ibid., 3. Modern anglers make a distinction between a "pole," which is usually just a stick with a line tied to the end, and a "rod," which typically is a professionally produced item complete with handle, reel, and small metal "guides" spaced along its length and through which the line is cast or retrieved.

21. Langford, *Discovery*, 12.

22. Lieutenant Gustavus C. Doane, "The report of Lieutenant Gustavus C. Doane upon the so-called Yellowstone Expedition of 1870," 41st Cong., 3d sess., Senate Executive Document 51 (Washington, D.C., 1871), 4.

23. Trumbull, "The Washburn Yellowstone Expedition," 432. Throughout this paper, comments on fish natural history, history, management, and related topics are based primarily on John D. Varley and Paul Schullery, *Yellowstone Fishes: Ecology, History, and Angling in the Park* (Harrisburg, Pa.: Stackpole Books, 1998). For additional information provided here on western native fishes, see Robert Behnke, *Native Trout of Western North America* (Bethesda, Md.: American Fisheries Society, 1992). Context on fishing history is provided primarily by Schullery, *American Fly Fishing.*

24. The earliest example of this suggestion that I have found was written by "G.A." in *The American Turf Register and Sporting Magazine* 3 (July 1832): 565. Discussing a day's fishing outing in New Hampshire, the writer said, "I soon ascertained that the patent English line and *artificial fly* would not do. Our fish are too Republican, or too shrewd, or too stupid, to understand the *science of English* Trout Fishing. I therefore took the common hook and worm, with a simple line and light sinker, and a rod cut on the spot; they then understood, and we readily caught in a short time, twenty-three fine *brook Trout*" (italics and capitalization as in the original).

25. Doane, "Report," 3.

26. Ibid.

27. Haines, *Yellowstone National Park*, 1:137–39. I am also indebted to Kim Allen Scott, Special Collections librarian, Montana State University Libraries, Bozeman, Montana, for a reading of his in-press manuscript biography of Doane.

28. Warren Gillette, "The Quest of Warren Gillette," ed. Brian Cockhill, *Montana The Magazine of Western History* 22, no. 3 (Summer 1972): 18.

29. Gillette, "Quest," 19.

30. For an expert angler opinion and commentary on the Yellowstone cutthroat as a sport fish and a comparison to the Snake River cutthroat, which is famous for its fighting

qualities, see Ernest Schwiebert, *Trout*, 2 vols. (New York: E. P. Dutton, 1978), 1:287–90, in which Schwiebert recounts conversations about cutthroat trout with famous Jackson Hole guide Bob Carmichael.

31. Langford, *Discovery*, 38.

32. Henry D. Washburn, "The Yellowstone Expedition, explorations in a new and wonderful country—description of the Great Falls of the Yellowstone—volcanic eruptions, spouting geysers, etc.," *Helena (Mont.) Daily Herald*, September 27, 28, 1871, quoted from reprint in Louis C. Cramton, *Early History of Yellowstone National Park and Its Relation to National Park Policies* (Washington, D.C.: U.S. Government Printing Office, 1932), 94.

33. Nathaniel Langford, "The Wonders of the Yellowstone," *Scribner's Monthly*, May 1871, 119.

34. Doane, "Report," 19.

35. James Pritchard, *Preserving Yellowstone's Natural Conditions* (Lincoln: University of Nebraska Press, 1990), 80.

36. Langford, "The Wonders of Yellowstone," 114.

37. Cornelius Hedges, "Yellowstone Lake," *Helena (Mont.) Daily Herald*, November 9, quoted in Cramton, *Early History of Yellowstone National Park*, 108–9. For variations on these stories, see also Hedges's letter to his sister, which includes the following passage: "The Lake itself is 25 miles long—we reached it first Sept. 3—I left it on the 17th having gone entirely around it—I caught hundreds of trout in its waters, the smallest one would weigh more than two pounds. . . . there are many hot springs around the lake & in some places in the very bottom of the lake—so close & so hot are some of these springs that one day I caught a large trout & in pulling him out he fell off my hook over a hot spring & before I could toss him out with my pole he was cooked thru." Cornelius Hedges to "Dear Sister," October 11, 1870, p. 3, SC 1974, Montana Historical Society Research Center,

Helena. For another account of Hedges's experience with the trout that fell into the hot spring, see Trumbull, "The Washburn Yellowstone Expedition," 492.

38. Hedges, "Diary," 9.

39. Ibid.

40. Lee Whittlesey's *Lost in the Yellowstone: Truman Everts's "Thirty-Seven Days of Peril"* (Salt Lake City: University of Utah Press, 1995) is the most thorough account of Everts's experience, including a complete version of his own published story.

41. Doane, "Report," 23.

42. Hedges, "Diary," 10. Note the mention of fishing on Sunday. See chapter 1, footnote 10, for a source of additional information on ambivalence about Sunday fishing.

43. Langford, *Discovery,* 83–84.

44. Doane, "Report," 27.

45. Hedges, "Diary," 11.

46. Ibid., 12.

47. Langford, *Discovery,* 116.

48. Gillette, on September 18, said, "Williamson left Moore & myself to make a shelter (which we did with poles & blankets) while he went out to hunt. In about an hour we heard him halou in the mountains. Heard his shots first. Moore took the mule & went to where we heard the shots & returned with a fine fat 2 year old heifer Elk. We ate the liver for supper. I must not forget that I killed another chicken today with my pistol, of which I feel quite proud." Gillette, "The Quest," 27.

49. Ibid., 29. Though historians have been aware of Gillette's journal mention of fly fishing for many years, to my knowledge the first fishing writer to point it out as the earliest known reference to the sport in Yellowstone was John Monnett, in *Cutthroat and Campfire Tales: The Fly-Fishing Heritage of the West* (Boulder, Colo.: Pruett Publishing Company, 1988),

49. This book, which I refer to here and there in the present book, deserves a much wider audience than it seems to have so far found, and as interest in western fishing history and western-fishing writing criticism grows, I hope to see it get that attention.

50. I admit that this is only a guess on my part. The rise of the fly fisher as a self-conscious "type" in the nineteenth century, especially in terms of the exclusivity of tackle use, has not been adequately explored by any writer. Based on my reading, I suspect that far more American trout fishermen in the 1830s were likely to readily shift among techniques than were their counterparts in the 1890s. This is to say that I assume that by the 1890s, there were, proportionately, many more anglers who fly fished as their primary or sole method than there had been in the 1830s. I explore some of the background for this possible transformation, from the generalist angler to the specialist, in *American Fly Fishing,* 32–42, 246–50.

51. For the most thorough compilation of wildlife observations by the Washburn Party, see Paul Schullery and Lee Whittlesey, "The Documentary Record of Wolves and Related Wildlife Species in the Yellowstone National Park Area Prior to 1882," in J. D. Varley and W. G. Brewster, eds., *Wolves for Yellowstone? A Report to the United States Congress, Volume IV, Research and Analysis* (Yellowstone National Park: National Park Service, 1992), 1.51–1.58.

52. Though none of the authors would likely approve of me describing their books quite in this way, it is easy enough, and quite helpful, to read Herman, *Hunting and the American Imagination*; Cartmill, *A View to a Death in the Morning*; and even Reiger, *American Sportsmen and the Origins of Conservation,* as chronicles of the evolving relationship between sport and subsistence, or leisure and survival, over the time periods covered in each book.

53. I consider the complications of catch-and-release fishing as it compares to traditional subsistence fishing in *Real Alaska*, 180–200.

54. A good discussion of the combination and interplay of sport and art in nineteenth-century North America is Karen Wonders, "Big Game Hunting and the Birth of Wildlife Art," in *Carl Rungius: Artist and Sportsman* (Toronto: Glenbow Museum and Warwick Publishing, 2001).

CHAPTER 4
YELLOWSTONE II

1. Edward Ringwood Hewitt, *A Trout and Salmon Fisherman for Seventy-Five Years* (New York: Van Cortlandt Press, 1972), 15. The original edition was published in 1948 by Scribner's, but the Van Cortlandt edition is essentially identical, so my page-number citations are interchangeable.

2. John Moldenhauer, *Rising Trout Sporting Books, Occasional List #21* (Hanover, Ontario, November, 2003), 4. This is an out-of-print sporting-book catalog with the book-dealer's commentary.

3. Both the *Newsweek* quote and the quote by Hewitt are from George Laycock, "Passing of a Great Fisherman," *The Fisherman*, May 1957, 31. Hewitt was renowned for many years, as shown by Marguerite Ives's account of him in *Seventeen Famous Outdoorsmen* (Chicago: Canterbury Press, 1929), 82–91.

4. The premier historical sources on Yellowstone Park are Haines, *The Yellowstone Story*; Bartlett, *Nature's Yellowstone*; and Richard A. Bartlett, *Yellowstone: A Wilderness Beseiged* (Tucson: University of Arizona Press, 1985).

5. Haines, *The Yellowstone Story*, 2:478.

6. Hewitt, *A Trout and Salmon Fisherman*, 15.

7. In 1882, Henry M. Teller was secretary of the Interior.

8. Edward Hewitt, *Those Were the Days* (New York: Duell Sloan and Pearce, 1943), 3.

9. P. H. Conger, *Annual Report of the Superintendent of the Yellowstone National Park to the Secretary of the Interior for the Year 1882* (Washington, D.C.: U.S. Government Printing Office, 1882), 9.

10. Hewitt's father and Sir John had not come all the way to the park; neither of them "felt up to making this long, hard trip" from an army encampment far down the Yellowstone Valley. Hewitt, *A Trout and Salmon Fisherman*, 15.

11. Ibid.

12. Lieutenant General P. H. Sheridan, *Report of an Exploration of the Parts of Wyoming, Idaho, and Montana in August and September, 1882, Made by Lieut. Gen. P. H. Sheridan, Commanding the Military Division of the Missouri, with the Itinerary of Col. Jas. F. Gregory, and a Geological and Botanical Report by Surgeon W. H. Forwood* (Washington, D.C.: U.S. Government Printing Office, 1882).

13. The Sheridan party itinerary is described in detail in Sheridan, *Report of an Exploration*, 5–18. According to Carroll Van West, in *Capitalism on the Frontier: Billings and the Yellowstone Valley in the Nineteenth Century* (Lincoln: University of Nebraska Press, 1993), 139, "the first Northern Pacific train pulled into Billings" on Tuesday, August 22, 1882.

14. Hewitt, *A Trout and Salmon Fisherman*, 15.

15. Ibid., 15–16.

16. If it mattered more to the story, I assume that it would not be impossible to track down the paperwork relating to this arrangement. A contingent of troops, sent off to escort a group of prominent citizens for several weeks, would necessarily have left a substantial paper trail in U.S. Army records.

17. Hewitt, *A Trout and Salmon Fisherman*, 16.

18. Ibid.

19. This is a common lament of visitors, and I suspect it is universal with many kinds of attractions. Now that I've been observing the Mammoth Hot Springs and other park features for thirty years myself, I've been at it long enough that I personally remember how they looked when some other visitor complains that they are sadly different. Different they may be, but not smaller or less colorful. Very few visitors, in fact, take enough time to get a reasonable grasp of the entire several-acre complex of springs and formations; they aren't in a position to judge whether the total flow of water, or total area of active algae growth, has changed. Reality just can't measure up to their lovingly embroidered memories.

20. Hewitt, *A Trout and Salmon Fisherman*, 16.

21. Charles Brooks, in "A Brief History of Fly Fishing in Yellowstone Park," *American Fly Fisher* 1, no. 4 (Fall 1974): 2–6, reviewed some of the most accessible historical sources on early fly fishing in the park, concluding that the Earl of Dunraven, in 1874, was the first fly fisher. As I show in chapter 3, it appears that members of the Washburn-Langford-Doane Expedition fly fished. I assume that quite a few other visitors must have also done so in the 1870s; they were on vacation trips, the park was already known for its hunting and fishing, and the fishing was easy. For more on the early history of fishing and fisheries management in Yellowstone, see Varley and Schullery, *Yellowstone Fishes*; and John Byorth, "Trout Shangri-La: Remaking the Fishing in Yellowstone National Park," *Montana The Magazine of Western History* 52, no. 2 (Summer 2002): 38–47.

22. Hewitt, *A Trout and Salmon Fisherman*, 16.

23. Ibid.

24. Lee Whittlesey, *Yellowstone Place Names* (Helena: Montana Historical Society Press, 1988), 53, 75. Excelsior Geyser was active through most of the 1880s and apparently occasionally erupted in the 1890s and until about 1901. In

the 1980s, it erupted more modestly, to a height of a few feet, but has not regained its explosive force of the 1880s.

The most complete history of Excelsior Geyser is Lee Whittlesey, "Monarch of All These Mighty Wonders: Tourists and Yellowstone's Excelsior Geyser, 1881–1890," *Montana The Magazine of Western History* 40, no. 1 (Spring 1990): 2–15.

Thanks also to Yellowstone's park historian, Lee Whittlesey, we also know a little bit more about the arrangements for the Bayard trip. Lee provided me with the text of an article that was written by George L. Henderson, an early park assistant superintendent and the first serious naturalist-interpreter to work in Yellowstone. The article, "Park Notes," appeared in the *Livingston (Mont.) Enterprise,* November 20, 1886. In it, Henderson reminisced as follows: "I witnessed the eruption of Excelsior in 1882, when Admiral Gorringe of the U.S.N. was making his tour of the park." Henderson gives the impression that this happened in September. Henderson could have been escorting the party in his capacity of assistant superintendent, or he could have been working for the party as a hired guide. In either case, his presence with Gorringe (and the unmentioned Edward Hewitt) further heightens my suspicion that the informality that Hewitt implies about the planning of the trip was not real. Henderson, whether guiding them officially or on his own time, was in fact the premier Yellowstone nature guide in the 1880s and 1890s; this was the beginning of that distinguished if forgotten career. The definitive portrayal of Henderson's career in Yellowstone is Lee Whittlesey, "The First National Park Interpreter: G. L. Henderson in Yellowstone, 1882–1902," *Montana The Magazine of Western History* 46, no. 1 (Spring 1996): 26–41.

25. Hewitt, *A Trout and Salmon Fisherman,* 17.

26. Again, I have never seen Bayard's name associated with this key campaign in the early conservation movement, while

other leading figures in the early conservation movement were known to have done the serious work in bringing about this momentous change in Yellowstone management. And again, though I will do some more looking into this question, I must assume that Hewitt was over-impressed with his party and their importance. In my book, *Searching for Yellowstone: Ecology and Wonder in the Last Wilderness* (1997; repr. Helena: Montana Historical Society Press, 2004), 68–88, I summarize this era in park wildlife management with particular attention to the slaughter of the large mammals and the possible effects of that "ecological holocaust." The disallowing of public hunting in the park was one of the most far-reaching developments in the long and eventful history of the national park idea. It instantly created what amounted to the world's foremost game reserve and forever changed the direction of national park management. Up to that point, Yellowstone's "important" resources were the static ones—the hydrothermal features, the scenery, the recreational opportunities. Suddenly, the wildlife itself was a primary visitor attraction, and wildlife, being mobile, "fugitive resources," placed a whole new set of demands on managers, who have spent the entire 120 years since then steadily refining their definition of how management should deal with such fluid elements of the landscape.

Interestingly, it was sportsmen who led the campaign to stop all public hunting in the park. Led by George Bird Grinnell (editor of *Forest and Stream* and co-founder with Theodore Roosevelt of the Boone and Crockett Club) and other like-minded sportsmen, they argued that as long as the park was protected, it would serve perpetually as a "game reservoir" from which animals would migrate to restock hunting lands beyond the park boundaries.

27. Hewitt, *A Trout and Salmon Fisherman*, 17.
28. Ibid.
29. Ibid., 17–18.

30. For more on the bigger picture of the rise of a conservation consciousness among American sportsmen, see Reiger, *American Sportsmen and the Origins of Conservation.*

31. Hewitt, *A Trout and Salmon Fisherman,* 18.

32. Ibid. Note also that Hewitt was eager to engage in the practice of boiling live fish in park hot springs, which Cornelius Hedges, twelve years earlier, had been appalled to do accidentally. See Varley and Schullery, *Yellowstone Fishes,* 5.

33. Hewitt, *A Trout and Salmon Fisherman,* 18. I'm only guessing here that he meant he traveled down the Firehole River from Old Faithful fifteen miles to its junction with the Gibbon River, where the Madison River begins, and then traveled down the Madison River another six miles. It is also possible that he thought that the river that flowed past Old Faithful, which was actually the Firehole River, was itself the Madison River. If this was the case, then he fished the Firehole River.

34. Ibid.

35. Varley and Schullery, *Yellowstone Fishes,* 93.

36. Haines, *The Yellowstone Story,* 2:478.

37. Ken Owens, "Fishing the Hatch," 10–19.

CHAPTER 5
DARK STONES AND DEVIL SCRATCHERS

1. George Newport [and possibly others], "The generic characters of Pteronarcys, etc.," *Proceedings of the Linnean Society of London,* vol. 1, November 1838 to June 1848 (R. and J. E. Taylor, 1849), June 20, 1848, 388.

2. Thanks to Richard Hoffmann, York University, Ontario, for providing me with this translation and other guidance.

3. Biographical information provided by Gena Douglas, librarian and archivist, Linnean Society of London, March 8, 2004.

4. Theodore Hartweg, "Journal of a Mission to California in Search of Plants," *Journal of the Horticultural Society of London,* 1 (1846), 180–85; ibid., 2 (1847), 121–25, 187–91; ibid., 3 (1848), 217–28.

5. Though Hartweg's account of his locations during his travels are often somewhat vague, a comparison of the route he describes in his narrative with the known distribution of *Pteronarcys californica* as provided by the U.S. Geological Survey's Northern Prairie Wildlife Research Center county-by-county map of the species' distribution suggests that both during his time near the coast, in the Monterey–San Francisco area, and during his travels inland, in the upper portions of the valleys of the Sacramento and Feather Rivers and Bear Creek, Hartweg could have been in currently known habitat of the giant stone fly. See http://www.npwrc.usgs.gov/resource/ distr/insects/ca/546.htm for "USGS/NPWRC Stoneflies of the United States, Stoneflies of California, Giant Salmonfly (*Pteronarcys californica*)."

6. George Newport, "On the anatomy and affinities of Pteronarcys regalis, Newm.: with a postscript containing descriptions of new American Perlidae, together with notes on their habits," *Transactions of the Linnean Society,* 20 (1851): 450. My thanks to Lawrence Currie, special use librarian, California Academy of Sciences, San Francisco, for alerting me to this later citation.

7. Monnett, *Cutthroat and Campfire Tales,* 58.

8. Kipling, *American Notes,* 200.

9. Mary Orvis Marbury, *Favorite Flies and Their Histories* (Boston: Houghton Mifflin Company, 1892).

10. Ibid.

11. Ibid., 455.

12. I discuss the rise of imitationists and imitation theory in the United States in *American Fly Fishing,* 83–121.

13. Philetus W. Norris, *Report of the Superintendent of the*

Yellowstone National Park (Washington, D.C.: U.S. Government Printing Office, 1881), 20.

14. Elwood Hofer, "Game in the Park," *Forest and Stream*, August 25, 1887, 88.

15. Richard A. Muttkowski, "The Food of Trout in Yellowstone National Park," *Roosevelt Wild Life Bulletin* 2, no. 4 (February 1925): 474–81.

16. The best source of historical information on Montana's older fly-tying traditions are George Grant, *Montana Trout Flies* (Portland, Ore.: Champoeg Press, 1981); and George Grant, *The Master Fly Weaver* (Portland, Ore.: Champoeg Press, 1980). Much of the following discussion is based on these two books, as well as on conversations with George Grant. See also George Grant, "Bunyan Bugs," *American Fly Fisher* 8, no. 3 (Summer 1981): 12–14. John Monnett's splendid *Cutthroat and Campfire Tales,* contains much talk about the evolution of western trout flies. Among the other helpful sources are Bud Lilly and Paul Schullery, *Bud Lilly's Guide to Fly Fishing the New West* (Portland, Ore.: Frank Amato, 2000); Antrim "Pat" Barnes with Dave Shors, *Ribbons of Blue: The Life and Lore of the "Old Pro" Pat Barnes* (Helena, Mont.: Helena Independent Record, 1997); and Charles F. Waterman, *Mist on the River: Remembrances of Dan Bailey* (Livingston, Mont.: Yellowstone Press, 1986). The Maclean quotation is from Norman Maclean, *A River Runs Through It and Other Stories* (Chicago: University of Chicago Press, 1976), 86.

17. This discussion of Don Martinez is based primarily on George Grant, "Don Martinez, Western Dry Fly Master," *American Fly Fisher* 9, no. 2, (Spring 1982): 8–14; the Martinez/Jennings letters in the Preston Jennings Collection, American Museum of Fly Fishing, Manchester, Vermont (hereafter Jennings Collection); and Martinez's fishing map, as cited in note 18.

18. Donald Martinez, "Fishing Guide," informational handout, 3d ed. (West Yellowstone, Mont.: Don's Tackle Shop, 1941); Don Martinez to Preston Jennings, January 3, 1940, Jennings Collection.

19. Grant, "Don Martinez," 14.

20. Don Martinez to Preston Jennings, November 23, 1941, Jennings Collection.

21. Barnes and Shors, *Ribbons of Blue,* 108–9.

22. Adele F. Jennings, "Our Trip West," *American Fly Fisher* 11, no. 2 (Spring 1984): 21.

23. George Grant, "Franz Pott: Western Original," *American Fly Fisher* 7, no. 2 (Spring 1980): 21.

24. Waterman, *Mist on the River,* 30–31.

25. Chris Cauble, "Early-day Anglers Took Lunkers to a Book Store," *Livingston (Mont.) Enterprise,* June 13, 1984, 9; Schullery, *American Fly Fishing,* 185.

26. Joseph Kinsey Howard, *Montana: High, Wide, and Handsome* (New Haven: Yale University Press, 1943), 85.

27. Grant, *Master Fly Weaver,* 7.

28. Grant, *Montana Trout Flies,* 139.

29. Marshall Riggen, *Three Men, Three Rivers,* VHS, directed by Mike Gurnett (Helena: Montana Fish, Wildlife and Parks, n.d.).

30. For the best summary of Grant's career, especially his conservation achievements, see Pat Munday, "'A millionaire couldn't buy a piece of water as good': George Grant and the Conservation of the Big Hole River Watershed," *Montana The Magazine of Western History* 52, no. 2 (Summer 2002): 20–37.

31. Grant, "Franz Pott," 22.

CHAPTER 6
A RIVER RUNS THROUGH IT AS FOLKLORE AND HISTORY

1. Gordon J. Brittan Jr., "Common Texts," in *American*

Authors Series: Norman Maclean, ed. Ron McFarland and Hugh Nichols (Lewiston, Idaho: Confluence Press, 1988), 182–89. I am happy to say that the present chapter, which was first prepared as the keynote talk given at the annual dinner of the Friends of the Montana State University Libraries, October 11, 2001, was in good part a response to the splendid collection of original Maclean writings, interviews, and critical essays in McFarland and Nichols's book. Though I first encountered some of the selections I cite below in earlier forms, it is simplest and most helpful to readers for me to cite them in their form in this book.

2. Ibid., 182.

3. Maclean, *A River Runs Through It,* 2.

4. Wallace Stegner, "Haunted by Waters," in *American Authors Series: Norman Maclean,* 157.

5. Wendell Berry, "Style and Grace," ibid.

6. Norman Maclean, "The Hidden Art of a Good Story: Wallace Stegner Lecture," ibid.

7. I used this moment from *A River Runs Through It* to make the same point in my *American Fly Fishing,* 184.

CHAPTER 7

COWBOY TROUT

1. For discussions of pre-Columbian human populations of the New World and what happened to those populations when Europeans and their diseases arrived, see David E. Stannard, *American Holocaust: The Conquest of the New World* (New York: Oxord University Press, 1992); Ann F. Ramenofsky, *Vectors of Death: The Archaeology of European Contact* (Albuquerque: University of New Mexico Press, 1987); William M. Denevan, *The Native Population of the Americas in 1492,* rev. ed. (Madison: University of Wisconsin Press, 1992); and David Henige, *Numbers from Nowhere:*

The American Indian Contact Population Debate (Norman: University of Oklahoma Press, 1998).

2. Richard Hoffmann, "Economic Development and Aquatic Ecosystems in Medieval Europe," *American Historical Review* 100, no. 3 (1996): 646.

3. Richard Hoffmann, "Environmental Change and the Culture of Common Carp in Medieval Europe," *Guelph Ichthyological Review* 3 (1995): 74–77.

4. Richard Hoffmann, "The Catch, Medieval European Fisheries and the Antecedents of Today's World Fisheries Crisis: An Essay in Environmental History," manuscript project proposal loaned by the author, 4.

5. Alfred Crosby, *Ecological Imperialism: The Biological Expansion of Europe, 900–1900* (London: Cambridge University Press, 1986). See also Alfred Crosby's *The Columbian Exchange: Biological and Cultural Consequences of 1492* (Westport, Conn.: Greenwood Press, 1972). For a variety of recent interpretations and opinions on what humans do to landscapes they either occupy for a long time or move into more abruptly, see Emily W. B. Russell, *People and the Land through Time: Linking Ecology and History* (New Haven: Yale University Press, 1997); and Tom Griffiths and Libby Robin, *Ecology and Empire: Environmental History of Settler Societies* (Seattle: University of Washington Press, 1997). I will warn you in advance, however, that these people, having (if you'll pardon the expression) bigger fish to fry, virtually never mention trout.

6. Thomas Dunlap, *Nature and the English Diaspora: Environment and History in the United States, Canada, Australia, and New Zealand* (London: Cambridge University Press, 1999), 54–59; Yvonne Baskin, *A Plague of Rats and Rubbervines: The Growing Threat of Species Invasions* (Washington, D.C.: Island Press, 2002), 19–37. This is not to say that the widespread movement of non-native species

began in the 1850s. It had long been underway, thanks to millennia of travelers, and in the case of European species, thanks to many ship captains who happily dropped off a variety of intentional (goats, pigs, etc.) and unintentional (rats, snakes) animal colonists in many places.

7. Arthur Nicols, *The Acclimisation of the Salmonidae at the Antipodes, Its History and Results* (London: Sampson, Low, Marston, Searle, and Rivingston, 1882), 2.

8. J. C. Mottram, *Fly-Fishing: Some New Arts and Mysteries* (London: Field and Queen [Horace Cox], 1915), 77.

9. Cecil Heacox, *The Complete Brown Trout* (New York: Winchester Press, 1974), 13. While visiting Cape Town on his famous voyage aboard the *Beagle*, Darwin noted that all across the southern hemisphere "little embryo Englands are springing to life in many quarters." Charles Darwin, *The Voyage of the Beagle* (New York: Penguin, 1989), 358.

10. Dunlap, *Nature and the English Diaspora*, 55.

11. See Nicols for one detailed first-hand telling of this adventure in scientific husbandry.

12. II. R. MacCrimmon and T. L. Marshall, "World Distribution of Brown Trout: *Salmo trutta*," *Journal Fisheries Research Board of Canada* 25, no. 12 (1968): 25–42.

For what is both a fascinating tale of fisheries management and the most thorough summary of the distribution of brook, brown, and rainbow trout that I have seen in the scientific literature, see all the papers by MacCrimmon and his colleagues, as follows: H. R MacCrimmon and J. S. Campbell, "World Distribution of Brook Trout, *Salvelinus fontinalis*," *Journal Fisheries Research Board of Canada* 26, no. 7 (1969): 1699–1725; H. R. MacCrimmon, B. L. Gots, and J. S. Campbell, "World Distribution of Brook Trout, *Salvelinus fontinalis*: Further Observations," *Journal Fisheries Research Board of Canada* 28, no. 3 (1971): 452–56; H. R. MacCrimmon and T. L. Marshall, "World Distribution of

Brown Trout, *Salmo trutta*," *Journal Fisheries Research Board of Canada* 25, no. 12 (1968): 2527–48; H. R. MacCrimmon, T. L. Marshall, and B. L. Gots, "World Distribution of Brown Trout, *Salmo trutta*: Further Observations," *Journal Fisheries Research Board of Canada* 27, no. 4: (1970): 811–18; H. R. MacCrimmon, "World Distribution of Rainbow Trout (*Salmo gairdneri*)," *Journal Fisheries Research Board of Canada* 28, no. 5 (1971): 663–704; H. R. MacCrimmon, "World Distribution of Rainbow Trout (*Salmo gairdneri*): Further Observations," *Journal Fisheries Research Board of Canada* 29, no. 12 (1972): 1788–91. This discussion is based primarily on the MacCrimmon papers, though it also relies on Robert Behnke, *Trout and Salmon of North America* (New York: Free Press, 2002); and Robert Behnke, "Brown Trout," *Trout* (Winter 1986): 42–47.

13. MacCrimmon, "World Distribution of Rainbow Trout," 688. For a fascinating account of how fly fishers have dealt with non-native trout and native-fish conservation issues in South Africa, with many helpful references to and comparisons with the U.S. experience, see Malcom Draper, "Going Native? Trout and Settling Identity in a Rainbow Nation," *Historia* 48, no. 1 (May 2003): 55–94.

14. Baskin, *A Plague of Rats and Rubbervines*, 3.

15. Roger R. Miller, James D. Williams, and Jack E. Williams, "Extinctions of North American Fishes during the Past Century," *Fisheries* 14, no. 6 (1989): 34. The authors point out that "of the forty taxa treated here, nineteen have disappeared since 1964." The problem is accelerating.

16. Varley and Schullery, *Yellowstone Fishes*, 119; Kurt D. Fausch, Christian E. Torgersen, Colden V. Baxter, and Hiram W. Li, "Landscapes to Riverscapes: Bridging the Gap between Research and Conservation of Stream Fishes," *BioScience* 52, no. 6 (June 2002): 483.

17. Behnke, *Trout and Salmon of North America*; Robert

Behnke, *Native Trout of Western North America* (Bethesda, Md.: American Fisheries Society Monograph 6, 1992) are my primary sources for fish status and distribution in North America. Another excellent source is Robert Smith, *Native Trout of North America*, rev. ed. (Portland, Ore.: Frank Amato Publications, 1995). For the Yellowstone situation, see Varley and Schullery, *Yellowstone Fishes*.

18. Behnke, *Trout and Salmon of North America*, 327.

19. John D. Varley and Robert E. Gresswell, "Ecology, Status, and Management of the Yellowstone Cutthroat Trout," *American Fisheries Society Symposium* 4 (1988): 14. For a fine popular account of the threats to the Yellowstone cutthroat, see Ted Williams, *The Insightful Sportsman* (Camden, Maine: Silver Quill Press, 1996), 283–91.

20. George A. Liknes and Patrick J. Graham, "Westslope Cutthroat Trout in Montana: Life History, Status, and Management," *American Fisheries Society Symposium* 4 (1988): 53; Behnke, *Trout and Salmon of North America*, 160–62.

21. David Quammen, "Planet of Weeds," *Harper's Magazine*, October 1998, 58–59.

22. Frank J. Rahel, "Homogenization of Fish Faunas across the United States," *Science* 288 (May 5, 2000): 856.

23. Charles Lose, *The Vanishing Trout: A Study of Trout and Trout Fishing in the Waters of Central Pennsylvania* (1931; repr., Baltimore: Gateway Press, 1993), 282.

24. I never expected to miss Richard Nixon, but the days when a landslide Republican president signed the Endangered Species Act into law look better all the time.

25. National Park Service, "Too Cool to Be Salmon—Glacier's Bull Trout," *Glacier Visitor Guide: The Official Newspaper of Glacier National Park,* Summer 2004, 3.

26. Delano Graff, e-mail message to author, February 22, 2000. Graff, a longtime fisheries manager and advocate in Pennsylvania, informed me of the Abele quote.

27. My thanks to philosopher Ned Hettinger for a conversation on the thorny issue of the sometimes shaky line between high-minded environmental purism and low-minded exclusionism. The following quote from Hettinger captures the uneasiness of this issue well: "But negatively evaluating a species simply because it is foreign smacks of xenophobia and a nativist desire to keep locals pure from 'foreign biological pollution.' In human affairs, such an attitude is morally repugnant. Nativist fear of foreigners and prejudice against immigrant peoples are morally troubling attitudes. Critics of biological nativism (i.e., the preference for native flora and fauna) point out that the Nazis had a native plant movement and attempted to purify the flora and fauna of their country as they purified their culture of Jews." Ned Hettinger, "Defining and Evaluating Exotic Species: Issues for Yellowstone Park Policy," *Western North American Naturalist* 61, no. 3 (2001): 257–60.

28. Luna B. Leopold, ed., *The Round River: From the Journals of Aldo Leopold* (London: Oxford University Press, 1953). Leopold's actual words were: "If the biota, in the course of aeons, has built something we like but do not understand, then who but a fool would discard seemingly useless parts? To keep every cog and wheel is the first precaution of intelligent tinkering. . . . Have we learned this first principle of conservation: to preserve all the parts of the land mechanism? No, because even the scientist does not yet recognize all of them" (pp. 146–47).

29. Bruce Farling, "Executive Director's Notes: A Native Obligation," *Trout Line: Newsletter from the Montana Council of Trout Unlimited*, Autumn 1999, 3.

30. This is more or less the point of my book *Searching for Yellowstone*. Take good care of something wild, and the longer you have it, the more it will serve you in ways that you don't yet have the wit to anticipate. For personal, senti-

mental, and thoughtful views of the worth of native trout in the West, see also Monnett, *Cutthroat and Campfire Tales,* 16–31; and M. R. Montgomery, *Many Rivers to Cross* (New York: Simon and Schuster, 1995).

31. It is true, however, that songbird conservation, as it arose in the late 1800s and early 1900s, did have a practical element. They were, at least many of them, insectivores, and were thus of value to agriculture because they helped protect crops from insect damage. Herman, *Hunting and the American Imagination,* discusses the involved sets of motives that often drove early conservation of non-game species.

32. Charles Gauvin, e-mail message to author, February 15, 2000.

CHAPTER 8
FLY FISHING AS IF IT MATTERS

1. An introduction to western water issues is Ed Marston, *Western Water Made Simple* (Washington, D.C.: Island Press, 1988).

2. Ken Owens, "While Custer Was Making His Last Stand: George Crook's 1876 War on Trout in the Bighorn Country," *Montana The Magazine of Western History* 52, no. 2 (Summer 2002): 58–61.

3. The need for a fuller accounting of the place of sport and the role of sportsmen in American historical studies has been eloquently pleaded for by others. See Thomas L. Altherr and John F. Reiger, "Academic Historians and Hunting: A Call for More and Better Scholarship," *Environmental History Review* 19 (Fall 1995): 39–56; Bantjes, "Introduction: Bourdieu on the Bighorn?" 2–5.

4. H. Duane Hampton's *How the U.S. Cavalry Saved Our National Parks* (Bloomington: Indiana University Press, 1971) serves as a foundation document for the involvement of the

army in conservation. Aubrey Haines's *The Yellowstone Story*; Bartlett's *Yellowstone*; and Sarah Broadbent, "Sportsmen and the Evolution of the Conservation Idea in Yellowstone" (M.A. thesis, Montana State University, Bozeman, 1997) all tell the story of the military's role in one especially important western wildlife conservation story.

5. From the earliest days of fly fishing in unsettled regions of North America, military sportsmen have been among the pioneering recreationists. Eastern Canada's trout and salmon rivers were of special interest to British officers in the early 1800s. See, for example, Schullery, *American Fly Fishing*, 49–51.

6. *Fly Fisherman, Fly Rod and Reel, Trout, Flyfisher, American Angler, Northwest Fly Fisher, The American Fly Fisher, Fly Tyer, Midwest Fly Fisher, The Art of Angling Journal, Saltwater Fly Fishing,* and *Fish & Fly* come to mind, but I am sure I have missed others. Many regional and local angling clubs also published periodically, everything from newsletters to full-fledged magazines; the most distinguished or venerable of these is the *Bulletin* of the Angler's Club of New York. In the West, *The Creel*, published by the Fly Fishers Club of Oregon since the 1960s, is a unique source of western fly-fishing lore.

Index

Page numbers in italics refer to photographs and illustrations.

About the author

Paul Schullery, a former director of the American Museum of Fly Fishing, is the author, co-author, or editor of more than thirty books on natural history, conservation, and sport. His previous fly-fishing-related books include *American Fly Fishing: A History* (1987); *Royal Coachman: The Lore and Legends of Fly Fishing* (1998); and *Shupton's Fancy: A Tale of the Fly Fishing Obsession* (1995). Paul has received numerous awards and honors, including an honorary doctorate of letters from Montana State University and the Wallace Stegner Award from the University of Colorado Center of the American West.